W9-BLW-630

Recruiting, Training, and Developing Volunteer Adult Workers

by
John Hendee

Illustrated by Rob Portlock

STANDARD PUBLISHING
Cincinnati, Ohio   18-88592

Acknowlwdgement
of permission to quote copyrighted material

The author is grateful to the authors and publishers who allowed him to use portions of their works in preparing this manual.

Ash, Mary Kay. *Mary Kay on People Management.* Copyright © 1984. Used by permission of Warner Books, New York, NY.

Callahan, Kennon. *Twelve Keys to an Effective Church.* Copyright © 1983. Used by permission of Harper & Row, Publishers, Inc., New York, NY.

MacDonald, Gordon. *Ordering Your Private World.* Copyright © 1984. Used by permission of Thomas Nelson Publishers, Nashville, TN.

Peters, Thomas J. and Nancy K. Austin, *A Passion for Excellence.* Copyright © 1985. Used by permission of Random House, Inc., New York, NY.

Peters, Thomas J. and Robert H. Waterman. *In Search of Excellence.* Copyright © 1982. Used by permission of Harper & Row, Publishers, Inc., New York, NY.

Smith, Fred. *Learning to Lead.* Copyright © 1986. Used by permission of Word Books, Publishers, Waco, TX.

White, John. *Excellence in Leadership.* Copyright © 1986. InterVarsity Press, Downers Grove, IL.

Unless otherwise noted, all Scripture quotations are from the *Holy Bible: New International Version,* ©1973, 1978, 1984 by the International Bible Society. Used by permission of Zondervan Bible Publishers and the International Bible Society.

Sharing the thoughts of his own heart, the author may express views not entirely consistent with those of the publisher.

Library of Congress Cataloging-in-Publication Data:

Hendee, John.
  Recruiting, training, and developing volunteer adult workers.
   1. Lay ministry—Recruiting. I. Title.
BV677.H46 1988   253.7   88-2255
ISBN 0-87403-442-6

Dedication

I'd like to dedicate this book to my family:
my wife Carla, my daughters Leah and Amber,
and my parents Wayne and Hazel Hendee.

What I have learned and am becoming is due in large part
to their support and love.

Purpose

This manual has been written for the purpose of giving direction in how to build a strategy for recruiting, training, and developing volunteer workers for the ministry of the church. The principles stated here apply to the work of the Sunday school and any number of other adult ministries in the church.

Contents

Introduction

There is no harder work in the life of the church than recruiting, training, and developing adult workers. Failure to give attention to this task is like assigning a congregation to a coma-like state; alive, but not functioning as designed.

We live in a day and age when a thousand things vie for the attention of those in the church. Time seems to be a commodity in short supply for everyone. Commitments are drawn to many things other than the cause of Christ. Sports, hobbies, and personal interests often seem to get in the way of doing what needs to be done for the Lord. Then there are the necessary physical, financial, emotional, familial, and other personal needs that demand time. Getting involved in ministries in the church often falls into the I-just-don't-have-time-for-that category.

"It happens whenever the pastor asks for volunteers."

The purpose of this book is to help you consider some factors that are involved in recruiting, training, and developing adult workers in the church, and to help you be more effective and successful in doing so.

After more than twenty years of working in the church, and spending most of that time in the field of Christian education, I have concluded that the task of recruiting, training, and developing adult workers is the make-or-break issue. I believe this issue drives more paid and volunteer leaders in the church to abandon leadership positions, or to turn those positions into simply holding the fort, than any other. I have talked to former church staff members who left their Christian education positions to preach at other churches because, as they put it, they couldn't wait to be free of the pressure of recruiting and training. I've seen leaders quit their positions, often angry with a church, because no one would help with a ministry.

This problem is the same in small churches and in large. No—actually, it gets harder the larger the church becomes. Recently, my wife and I went to a small church in northern Arizona. We were sitting in a small Sunday-school class of about twelve adults. The lesson was about serving the Lord. The discussion led to various class members' expressing their frustration over people in their church who would not take on jobs or would quit too soon or would not follow through on what they were supposed to be doing. At one point, the teacher turned toward us and said, "I'm sure you don't have all these kinds of problems, coming from such a big church with all those people." My wife and I just looked at each other and smiled.

We all have the same basic kinds of problems when it comes to recruiting, training, and developing adult workers. But we need not throw in the towel. We must decide this is a task that must be done. We will do it even though it is tough and is never finished.

My hope and prayer is that this book will help you in the challenging struggle ahead of you in building a corps or team of committed, competent, functioning adult workers in the church.

Chapter 1

The Purpose of Adult Ministries

As I reflect back on the controversy of the Vietnam war, it seems to me that during the conflict and the days to follow, the biggest question was, "Why were we there?" Few if any had a real sense of mission to explain why we were allowing men and women to die by the thousands. It was so different from World War II. After the bombing of Pearl Harbor, there was no question why we were sending troops to fight. We had been attacked.

Admiral Alfred T. Mahan of the American Navy is said to have insisted on this rule when teaching his officers: "Gentlemen, whenever you set out to accomplish anything, make up your mind at the onset about your ultimate objective. Once you have decided on it, take care never to lose sight of it."[1] General George Patton demanded that his men know and be able to articulate exactly what the current mission was. "What is your mission?" he would frequently ask. The definition of the mission was the most important piece of information a soldier could carry into combat. Based on that knowledge, he could make his decisions and implement the plan.[2]

I believe a major factor for many churches' having weak or failing adult ministries is that the troops don't understand what their mission is or what their responsibility is.

Surely you have heard about the administration of God's grace that was given to me for you, that is, the mystery made known to me by revelation, as I have already written briefly. In reading this, then, you will be able to understand my insight into the mystery of Christ, which was not made known to men in other generations as it has now been revealed by the Spirit to God's holy apostles and prophets. This mystery is that through the gospel the Gentiles are heirs together with Israel, members together of one body, and sharers together in the promise in Christ Jesus.

I became a servant of this gospel by the gift of God's grace given me through the working of his power. Although I am less than the least of all God's people, this grace was given me: to preach to the Gentiles the unsearchable riches of Christ, and to make plain to everyone the administration of this mystery, which for ages past was kept hidden in God, who created all things. His intent was that now, through the church, the manifold wisdom of God should be made known to the rulers and authorities in the heavenly realms, according to his eternal purpose which he accomplished in Christ Jesus our Lord. In him and through faith in him we may approach God with freedom and confidence (Ephesians 3:2-12).

The church has a tremendous task ahead of it. It is a task for which the world waited hundreds of years to see. It is a task that was planned for the church before history began. It is a task the angels knew of, but only the church could carry out. Abraham dreamed of it. Isaiah and others preached of it. Jesus delivered it, and initiated it. The church is to carry it out and finish it. The task is to administrate the New Covenant.

How do you measure whether you are effectively administering the New Covenant? There are two questions you need to ask. First, "Are we growing in numbers?" Numerical growth is not unspiritual. The Bible records the numerical growth of the early church.

Those who accepted his message were baptized, and about three thousand were added to their number that day (Acts 2:41).

And the Lord added to their number daily those who were being saved (Acts 2:47).

But many who heard the message believed, and the number of men grew to about five thousand (Acts 4:4).

And so it continues throughout the book of Acts.

The second question is, "Are we growing in Christlike character." Paul was concerned with Christlike growth.

Then we will no longer be infants, tossed back and forth by the waves, and blown here and there by every wind of teaching and by the cunning and craftiness of men in their deceitful scheming.

Instead, speaking the truth in love, we will in all things grow up into him who is the Head, that is, Christ. From him the whole body, joined and held together by every supporting ligament, grows and builds itself up in love, as each part does its work (Ephesians 4:14-16).

Thus the **purpose** of adult ministries is to help advance the cause of Christ as spelled out in the New Covenant. The purpose of the New Covenant is to bring men and women into a peace relationship with God and others. It is to provide salvation through the offer of Christ. The church must be busy helping to fulfill this cause. There is a lot of talk about doing so, but little of the activity expended by many churches actually is in this direction. Our task in recruiting, training, and developing adult workers in the church is to help them become more effective in carrying out this task. We must get some positive results. We are commanded to. To do less is to fail the Lord. Results will vary from one situation to the next, but the servant of Christ is called to produce fruit (converts) and to help them grow in Christlikeness.

If I don't have this purpose clear, I will find myself absorbed in meaningless activities or, at best, in simple maintenance. Rather than holding forth the Word of God, I will be holding forth the traditions of the local congregation, not doing anything or risking anything that might stir the waters. That is boring ministry. That kind of ministry kills Christian spirit, enthusiasm, and commitment.

It distorts Christian mission. It is a betrayal of the cause of Christ. It is sin of the most righteous-looking kind.

As leaders in the church, we must examine what we are doing. Are we seriously putting our energy into carrying out the mission, or are we just holding each other's hands? Are the programs we are carrying on and starting up really helping accomplish the goals Jesus had in mind for the church? Do our budgets reflect this? Does the monthly church calendar reflect it? We are to be recruiting, training, and developing adult workers for the task of the kingdom! Let's give it our best effort.

If our people don't understand the mission and if they aren't sold on it, it will be next to impossible to recruit, train, and develop them in ministry.

The Priority of Adult Ministries

A few years ago, I was speaking at Pacific Christian College in Fullerton, California, where Dr. Medford Jones introduced me to Dr. Elwyn Buche. As he did, he mentioned that I was the Minister of Evangelism and Christian Education at Central.* They then went on a minute or two talking about how rare that combination is among staff members of churches. I was a bit surprised with their conversation. As I had more time to think about it, I concluded that one reason so many churches aren't growing is that staff members and lay members in the church have too many jobs they don't combine with evangelism.

Education that doesn't have evangelism as a high priority and a major feature of its nature isn't Christian education. When I talk of the priority of adult ministries, I am suggesting that the highest priority must be evangelism in word and deed and program. That is, programming must be done with the needs and concerns of the non-Christian in mind. Too many adult programs in churches are put together with no other concerns than the needs of the church members. Dr. LeRoy Lawson regularly repeats the

thought that the church is the only institution on earth that exists for those who aren't part of it yet. That is the Great Commission at its heart. Yet so much of adult education tends to get bogged down in focusing only on the needs of those who have been in the church for ages. I suppose that is one reason I have had a hard time over the past few years with the emphasis on "discipling." I'm all for getting together one on one, especially with new Christians, and studying and praying together for the sake of growth. But the idea propagated in recent years seems to have been almost to the exclusion of evangelism. It ignores evangelism in one's personal life and in the mission and programming of the church as well.

Win Arn, in his book *The Master's Plan for Evangelism*, suggests a brilliant way for churches to program. The usual way is to think like this: "Let's plan a backpacking outing. We have a few people who like to be backpack. We can go for three days and have campfire devotions at night—it could be good fellowship." Arn suggests a better way. Rather than

---

*i.e. Central Christian Church, Mesa, Arizona, where the author continues to serve, now in the area of administration.

finding out the interests of the church members and then planning activities just for them, he suggests churches find out the interests of their members' closest friends or acquaintances, and program for them. For example, if there are fifteen friends or acquaintances of church members who like to backpack, then the church should plan a backpacking trip with the goal in mind of having members invite their friends on the outing. It could be just the kind of activity that the people can invite non-Christians to and get positive results. Let them get to know some other Christians. They might discover a little about the congregation and learn something about Jesus, too. It wouldn't be wise to have four hours of Bible study for every hour backpacking—one has to be smart in planning the activity—but the event could be used effectively for outreach. If a church gets Christians involved in outreach, it is doing the best thing it can to nurture and help them grow.

We must keep the **vision** of the church in focus. If you give all your attention to the needs of the church members, you will just be holding the fort, or you will be dying. If the church gives major evangelistic attention to the outsider and to reaching them, it will grow. You will also be concerned about taking care of your own people.

A church must be willing to count the cost if it makes the decision to keep evangelism a high priority in its adult ministries. We have made many decisions at Central with the non-Christians in mind. This does not always make some Christians happy. Some have left our fellowship because we have dared to do something differently for the sake of evangelism. If we believe a particular program or ministry will help us reach people and draw them closer to Christ, we will do it—even if it may mean losing some members.

We may need to ask and evaluate, "Are most of our programs for Christians? Is very much done to attract the outsider? Do we design events with the idea of helping our members feel comfortable inviting non-Christians to them?" We can be pretty narrow in our thinking about how to reach people. The growing church will be creative, flexible, and energetic without yielding Biblical convictions. It will program for evangelism.

"Good Morning"

Praying for Adult Ministries

Anything you are doing in your adult ministries deserves praying for. Our prayer life is one of the avenues that has the possibility of keeping our programming anchored to the will of the Lord. If we are honest with the Lord, we will keep the needs of the non-Christian on our hearts and in our activities. If we bring everything to the Lord and bathe it in prayer, we will last longer in carrying out the project because we will experience more of His sustaining power. We won't give up as quickly when the going gets tough. We are more likely to see some exciting results.

John White makes some interesting comments about prayer and planning.

Prayer is where planning starts. Our first goal in prayer is not to get a steamhead of power but to find out what God wants. Planning that arises from and is the product of prayer is far superior to planning that is merely "backed by" prayer.[3]

We are partners with God in all we do. We must take our dreams, needs, and ministries to Him for approval, examination, and support. We need to go to Him and seek ideas and dreams that go beyond our imaginations, limited visions, and desires.

Jesus said to pray to the Lord of the harvest that He might raise up workers. We must continue our thinking about recruiting, training, and developing adult workers by reminding ourselves that God has more at stake in our ministries than we do. We must not rush into all our activities without going to our King and seeking His aid in finding willing workers for His cause. He will help. That doesn't mean we won't have to put in hard work. But He will help raise up workers. The one condition that comes with His promise is that those workers be used to help bring in the harvest, not just keep the barn clean! If we try to recruit people just to maintain the barn, I'm not sure God is going to be as concerned about sending potential workers our way.

The Pride in Adult Ministries

In the past year, I have read four different books with the word *excellence* or *excellent* in the title: *In Search of Excellence, A Passion for Excellence, In Pursuit of Excellence,* and *Excellence in Leadership.* There is a lot of attention and concern today about excellence in all we do. The business world is giving major attention to it as it applies to building a successful company.

As we talk about recruiting, training, and developing volunteer adult workers for the church, we can be reminded that Jesus and Paul were concerned about excellence, too. All too often, we in the church have done things in a rather shoddy way, and we've got results that match. If we are going to ask people to give their lives in ministry for two hours a week, we must show them that what we are asking them to be a part of is important by the way we approach them to help us. We will talk about that later.

Paul said the following about quality and excellence:

Whatever you do, work at it with all your heart, as working for the Lord, not for men, since you know that you will receive an inheritance from the Lord as a reward. It is the Lord Christ you are serving (Colossians 3:23, 24).

Having pride in our ministries means doing things in the most effective, polished way we know how.

The authors of *A Passion for Excellence* say, "Excellence is a game of inches, or millimeters. No one act is, per se, clinching. But a thousand things, a thousand thousand things, each done a tiny bit better, do add up to memorable responsiveness and distinction—and loyalty."[4] Having pride in our work for Christ will result in seeking to do everything "a tiny bit better."

The same authors said the following about successful businesses,

In the private or public sector, in big business or small, we observe that there are only two ways to create and sustain superior performance over the long haul. First, take exceptional care of your customers (for chicken, jet engines, education, health care, or baseball) via superior service and superior quality. Second, constantly innovate.[5]

Doing our work with pride means it's not enough just to take care of your visitors, prospects, teachers, and sponsors. It means taking exceptional care of them.

A man of Jewish background visited our services some time back. When I followed up on him, he asked me, "Did you guys have some professionals come in and show you how to run everything?" What he was referring to were the things we were doing to try and help our visitors feel comfortable and at home. And it was noticed. We hadn't had any professionals come in. We were just trying to do a professional job in taking care of the people with whom we had contact.

The issue isn't having to do things in an expensive or extravagant way. This is not to say that most things we do wouldn't benefit by our spending more money on them, but money is not the concern. Whether with little money or much, we try to do things in a proper, excellent way. We are seeking to honor the Lord and carry out His cause in the best way we can.

The Prospects of Adult Ministries

Before you get carried away with running after adults to recruit and train, it would be good to consider the prospects for your ministries. Whom are you trying to reach? While it's true that evangelism is a priority in your programming, some of your programs will still basically focus on the needs of the people of the congregation. In order to plan those ministries, you need to do some basic homework so that you know how to minister to the groups the programs are supposed to serve.

First, you need to make sure you know your congregation. That may require that you do some basic study and surveying of your people to discover their makeup. What is the age breakdown of your people? How many retired people do you have? How many widows, newlyweds, and singles? Think of as many categories as you can—how many people are in each? You must know your people before you can program to meet their needs.

Second, you need to know your community. You can usually find demographic studies in public libraries. Often banks, local city departments, and realtors will also have studies or surveys of the community. It would be good to get and become familiar with some of these studies. Don't assume you know everything there is to know about your area. What is the demographic composition of your community by race, economics, age, and other factors? Being aware of the basic nature of your area will help you in planning to meet the needs of the people.

Third, you must keep in mind the difference between your non-Christian neighbors and your neighbors who are active in a church. The non-Christian neighbors may well be nice people, but at present they are not at all interested in church. They may think churches are just after people's money. Some of them use any and every holiday they can find as an excuse for a party, perhaps even a time to get drunk and let it loose. There is a drastic difference between those people and those who are active in a church. The latter are busy in many activities related to their congregation.

You have two extreme situations here. A church must be creative in seeing how to program for both. "For the people of this world are more shrewd in dealing with their own kind than are the people of the light" (Luke 16:8). In Matthew 10:16, Jesus told His disciples, "Therefore be as shrewd as snakes and as innocent as doves." When we apply this to our work with prospects, it means we must use our brains in the way we approach, contact, and relate to the outsiders. We don't approach them the way we would approach another Christian, or we may scare them off. Our programming must be sensitive to the outsider.

The issue here is, "How do you take care of your prospects once you get contact with them? How do you treat your customer?" Some might take objection with the word *customer*, but those who are your prospects are your "spiritual customers." Many are church shopping. They are looking for life. The big question is, "Will they find it in your group's presence?" You won't get them all to join you, but you must look like a good place to search or they will not stay, and you won't reach any. All this should lead you to examine how visitors are received when they walk into your activity.

We recently discovered something interesting at Central. When we moved into our new facility, our worship service grew rapidly. But our various departments and ministries didn't grow at the same pace as the worship service did. In studying this and trying to figure out why, one obvious reason popped out in front of us. We had worked hard at seeing that we took care of people when they visit our worship services. Here's a list of the things we've done to help people (our customers) when they visit the first time on a Sunday morning:

1. We provide parking attendants to help people in the parking lot.
2. We have greeters outside on the sidewalks, with maps and directories.
3. We have greeters in the foyer.
4. We have ushers to give people bulletins and help them find seats.
5. We ask everyone to stand at one point in the service and introduce themselves to those around them.
6. We give every visitor a guest packet at the end of each service, morning and evening.

7. If a visitor filled out a registration card, which we ask all in the service to do, we will put him on our mailing list and send him our newsletter.

8. Visitors will get a letter that week from our preacher.

9. Someone from the church will phone each first-time visitor on Monday night and let him know we are glad he visited us.

10. If he is interested, the person who phoned will visit in the visitor's home, and try to set up three additional evangelistic studies.

11. If we visit someone, we will give him a packet with a book and other materials on the church.

That is the basic list. We have seen the response of people who visit and are impressed with the attention given to them. It opens doors.

Now after being in our new building and seeing our growth in worship but not the other areas, the question came to mind, "What happens when people visit a Sunday-school class, or Children's Chapel, or choir rehearsal, or the Singles on Monday night, or the College-age group on Wednesday night? In comparison, very little. We will usually try and greet them, introduce them, and invite them back. That was basically it. So if people visited our worship service and another program area, to which of the two would they return? Obviously to the worship service. They didn't even have to sit down to analyze why. They were taken better care of there.

This has led us to start building ways to see that all our "customers" get special attention, without trying to embarrass them, whenever they attend any ministry area. Give some thought to how you are taking care of guests before, during, and after they attend your events.

By now, you may be wondering what this has to do with recruiting, training, and developing adult workers. Very much, actually. If the people you are trying to recruit can't see the vision, the big picture, the importance of what you are asking them to be a part of, they are less likely to want to be a part of it. You won't likely recruit them. But if they can see you are doing things right, that they will be a part of carrying out God's plan, that you are really interested in taking care of people, that people are more important than programs, that you aren't self-centered as a church, then it is more reasonable to believe that they would want to join you in your ventures for the Lord. They will be more willing to give of their time, energy, and money.

Notes

[1]John White, *Excellence in Leadership* (Downers Grove: IVP, 1986), p. 73.

[2]Gordon MacDonald, *Ordering Your Private World* (Nashville: Nelson, 1984), pp. 181, 182.

[3]White, *Excellence in Leadership*, p. 40.

[4]Tom Peters, Nancy Austin, *A Passion for Excellence* (New York: Random House, 1985), p. 46.

Chapter 2

Programming for Adult Ministry

There are many possibilities for adult programs that must be considered. We live in a hectic, fast-paced culture that places many demands on its people and offers a variety of ways to meet their needs and pleasures. When we go to the grocery store to buy soup, we don't have to take just one kind of soup. There are a variety of brands and styles. Dried, canned and ready to eat, canned and needing water added, and some that come in a cup and are ready in two minutes when you add hot water. People like choices. You don't have just one TV or radio station. There are dozens. If you don't like one, turn the dial.

It is the same in the work of the church. People are looking for more ways to learn and grow than just one program. A church that doesn't offer a variety of ways to meet the needs of its people will likely not grow to its potential. A church that doesn't offer a different menu of opportunities to its members and prospects will stifle its mission. A generic brand church in a yellow wrapper, with a "take it as it is" attitude won't impact our culture.

If there is a facility for it on or off campus, I believe a church is wise to run with a full-fledged Sunday school program. Sunday school can be one of the most powerful ministries in your adult program. It is one of the easiest programs to set up, operate, and build in most congregations. The time is right—the people are already there for worship services. There is provision for their children. It is convenient for most. It provides an excellent place to build small groups, which are essential for growth in a church. There are many churches with Sunday schools that are not growing, but that doesn't diminish the potential for Sunday school. But beyond Sunday school, a church must be looking for a variety of different programs to use to help reach and teach people for the Lord.

I need to take a moment to comment on what a "program" is in my mind. A program is any kind of plan and/or organization that is designed to meet valid needs of prospects or members of the church in light of the mission of the church. A program that isn't meeting valid needs of people is a waste of time, no matter how long a church has been doing it. Kennon Callahan makes some interesting comments about programs:

In this country, the preoccupation of local congregations with programs and activities is deplorable. People win people to Christ; programs do not. People discover people in significant relational groups, not in a merry-go-round of programs and activities.

Some churches become so involved in sponsoring a vast array of programs and activities that they lose sight of the people those programs and activities allegedly serve.[1]

This reminds us that while we need programs, we must make sure that they are continuing to meet genuine spiritual and other needs of people. Develop the attitude that programs are people, not plans on paper or a quarterly teacher's booklet. A program can be no better than our mission, our plan, and the people who are carrying it out.

Once Sunday school is in place and functioning, how does a church decide what other programs it could start? Callahan has some other excellent comments on this issue.

Once a congregation has claimed its strengths, it is strategic that it decide on new ways to expand these strengths. It is decisive in successful long-range planning that a congregation build on its strengths, not its weaknesses.... Strengths that are not used weaken and decay.

A church must "run to its strengths." In professional football, for a winning team to run to its strengths means that a team that has an all-pro right guard, right tackle, right end, and a right halfback will run to its right—that is, run to its strengths. Too many churches with strengths at "right guard, right tackle, right end, and right half-back" spend too much time trying to run plays around left end. They wonder why they don't have many "winning games." They run to their weaknesses rather than to their strengths.[2]

A congregation needs to ask "What are the needs of the community?" "What are the needs of the members of the church?" "What new programs can we implement to meet these needs?" Robert Schuller's motto of "find a need and meet it" is excellent when the church is looking for how it can carry out its mission. Of course, the priority given to meeting any or all of the various needs should be done in view of the mission of the church, that is, reaching the lost and leading the Christians into Christlikeness.

An example of how not being aware of the needs of the people around you can result in the death of a church is seen in a congregation I visited in the east. It was a congregation with a grand history. It is presently a shell of what it used to be. The congregation is now running about fifty in worship. They are immediately across the street from one of the largest universities in the east. They have old facilities, but they are in good condition. They have been maintained well. They could hold a congregation of three to four hundred people. One afternoon, I was standing in the sanctuary with a previous preacher of the church picturing the church's dying situation and thinking of what might be done to help it get growing again. I asked the former preacher if anyone had investigated the possibility of starting a preschool as a way to make contact with young married students on the campus. I figured there were probably 5000 or so young married students, many of whom could surely benefit from good but inexpensive child care right next to the campus. From there, the church could start an active young couples' ministry, and the possibilities would continue to grow. The man responded that that had been proposed, but the trustees voted it down. He then told me that once a senior citizens' group in the area has asked if they could rent the fellowship hall (which sits empty during the week) for three or four hours each weekday. They would eat together, make crafts, and hold meetings and programs. They had also asked if they could put a pool table in there. When the trustees heard that, they voted it down.

Then I suggested that they could use the fellowship hall as a light lunch and study hall for the students, and start a campus outreach. No, the man said, the trustees wouldn't go for that. At that point I was mad. "Wait a minute!" I said. "Do those guys own this church? Is this their building? Who do they think they are? This is God's building and it is to be used to reach people for Jesus. They're acting as if it is their job to protect the building from them!"

He already knew that. But it is that kind of protectionism in many churches that leaves them in the category of the steward who buried his talent. He lost it all in the end. And he thought he was being so faithful. He was a fool.

What are some specific programs, beyond Sunday school, then, that can be started up to meet the needs of your people? They are legion. There are as many

as you can find needs of people. Your church must pick a few and run with them till you grow enough to take on more. We are doing things today at Central Christian that we wanted to do years ago. But we didn't have the manpower, resources, or facility to do some of them then. We have dreams and plans of more things we want to do in the next five to ten years. We would like to be doing them now, but we have to grow into them.

Let me share with you some of the different programs we have adopted here at Central to try and meet the needs we saw in our ministry and mission. Many of these programs have evolved into their present status over months or years of development. We are researching other programs that we hope to implement in the future; others are just now beginning.

The Ambassador Training Program

We knew we needed to do a better job following up on our prospects. A good Sunday-school program or worship service without a good means to follow up on your prospects seriously limits you. It is like inviting people to your restaurant, showing them a tempting, picture-filled menu, but never coming to the table to take their orders. The Ambassador Training Program is a program we started several years ago to meet that need. It is now published by Standard Publishing and is available for other churches to use in training their people for calling on prospects and sharing the gospel with those who need it and are interested. We had a need, and we took a few years to figure how to meet it. In meeting our need, we found the program could be used by others as well to help them meet their evangelistic needs.

Center for Biblical Service (C.B.S.)

Some years back, we saw the need to train our people in many areas of ministry and help build their knowledge and ministry skills in many areas that we could never deal with in Sunday school. So we developed a program called C.B.S., the Center for Biblical Service. We presently run this program on Sunday nights before our evening service. (When we began the progam, we offered the classes on Sunday mornings, but we had to move it to Sunday evening when we were relocating. Eventually, we will return the program to Sunday mornings because we have found that we get more involvement then than on Sunday nights.)

We offer about ten different classes every six weeks. Most classes are seven weeks long; some are fourteen. Three Sunday nights of the year, we don't have any classes. We offer about forty different class subjects over the year.

The purpose of these classes is to equip our people for the work of the ministry. We want to get them involved in serving. We use our own people to teach these classes, although a church planning a similar program could bring people in from other churches to teach some classes if it needed or wanted to do so. We also use video studies.

We have a certificate program set up so people are working toward a Certificate of Ministry. There are required classes and electives. Here is a list of some of the topics:

How to Be a People Helper
The Life of Christ
Christian Leadership Principles
How to Plan a Successful Ministry
Creative Hospitality as a Means of Evangelism
Life-style Evangelism
Preparing and Delivering a Talk, Devotion, or Meditation
Christian Family Goals in Parenting
The Holy Spirit
Managing Yourself
Teacher Training
Music Leadership Training
Pastoral Care Training

Family Circles

Family Circles are our home Bible-study program, but the program goes way beyond being just a home Bible study. Our hope is that these groups will also be reaching out and that they will care for each other as a loving family. When they experience joys, they celebrate together; when they suffer, they support and help each other.

At present, we have about forty Family Circles. We hope to have in the hundreds some day. The circles average in size from eight to eighteen and meet on different nights of the week in homes of the circle members.

To become a Family Circle leader, a person must first participate in our training program. That person must also be willing to meet with all the other leaders every Sunday night before our evening service. This meeting prepares the leaders for leading their circle meetings during the following week.

This is the way the program works. Each week, Dr. Lawson is videotaped presenting the lesson material. That tape is brought to the Sunday evening meeting of leaders, where each leader gets a copy and is trained in how to use it to lead the discussion in the circle meeting. On the designated night, each

"I am Harvey's attorney.
He will agree to be a volunteer in your adult ministries program
as long as he gets the following: a break every 15 minutes, his
own dressing room with coffee and doughnuts provided, and an
engraved stone monument in front of the church building
recognizing his efforts."

Family Circle meets, views the videotape, and discusses the issues presented. There is also a time of prayer and sharing.

The subject matter varies, but for three months, the circles engage in what we call an "Us" study. Every fourth month is spent in a "Them" study. An Us study is a Bible study designed for Christians or people openly and enthusiastically interested in Bible study. The Them study is a special video series designed with the outsider, the non-Christian, in mind. We hope this will provide our people with good opportunities to invite their non-Christian friends and neighbors. The Them studies cover themes like family life, rearing teenagers, money management, and success. We hope that these studies will allow us to build some bridges to reach these people and provide an opportunity to share Christ with them.

The Stephen Series

The Stephen series is a program we have only recently begun. We did not develop it ourselves, but we picked it up because we believe it is the kind of program and resource that will help us meet the needs of people. Information on this program can be obtained from Stephen Ministries, 1325 Boland, St. Louis, MO, 63117. It is designed to involve the congregation in meeting the needs of the hospitalized, the terminally ill, the elderly, the disabled and handicapped, the shut-ins, the institutionalized, those in job crisis, and the lonely and depressed. It begins with the selection of a couple of people from your congregation to become "Stephen Leaders." They are then sent to a two-week "Leaders Training Course." After they are trained, they recruit and select members of the church. The leaders provide fifty hours of training to the recruits and then commission them as "Stephen Ministers." These new Stephen Ministers are in contact with people with special needs, and they do what they can to meet those needs.

One thing I have noticed about a growing church, and I believe it is a must for growth, is a willingness to innovate, experiment, and fail. For every program we have that has worked, we have probably had four or five programs that didn't work. A church that isn't willing to do anything unless it can be guaranteed that the program will work has no vision. It is a church weak in faith.

Again, you're wondering, "What does this have to do with recruiting, training, and developing adult workers in the church?" Simply this: before you can recruit, you have to know the ministry to which you are recruiting people. You need to plan out your programs and ministries in order to know your personnel needs. You will then know for what you are recruiting them, how you will train them, and how you will develop and support them. If you don't consider the possibilities, you will limit the potential for your church and for your people individually.

Notes

[1]Kennon L. Callahan, *Twelve Keys to an Effective Church* (San Francisco: Harper and Row, 1983), p. 39.

[2]Callahan, *Twelve Keys*, p. xvii.

Chapter 3

Determining the Positions for Effective Adult Ministry

Once you have figured out what programs you want, you need to develop a series of adult ministry job flow charts. First, develop the overall chart, and then design one for each program in the department. Job flow charts are very helpful tools. We require all of our staff members to update the job flow charts for their departments every year.

There are several advantages to a job flow chart:

1. It makes you account for all the tasks that need to be taken care of in any program.
2. It helps you determine how many people you need to carry out the tasks.
3. It helps you evaluate whether you are evenly distributing the work loads.
4. It will show you whether you have too few or too many people in the organization.
5. It helps you draw up lines of responsibility and accountability.
6. It makes you annually examine whether you are enlarging your organization, which is essential for steady growth.
7. It helps you see whether you are always using the same people or are bringing new people in and up in the program organization.
8. It will show you how you are doing in recruiting people to fill the positions in your organization.

There are a few principles I have discovered over the years that I think are worth pointing out in regard to our thinking about organizing a program.

Avoid the "Baby Shower Philosophy"

We tend to try and get by with too few helping out in most programs. Several years ago, while I was serving another congregation, I observed what I call the "baby shower philosophy" of programming. I was teaching a young couples class that went through a period of time when it seemed as if half the women in the class were pregnant. We had a baby shower almost every other week. The ladies who were sponsoring most of these learned the hard way how not to put on a baby shower. Here is how they started. Two of them would get together and plan a shower for the expectant mother. One would be in charge of invitations and decorations. The other would be in charge of refreshments and games. They would put a lot of time and money into getting

everything ready. The event was always well planned.

The night of the shower, they would be at the place with everything ready. The guest of honor would show up, and her mother would usually be with her. Then two or maybe three others would show up. Everyone would eagerly wait for more to arrive, but no one ever did. A couple gifts would have been dropped off, but no more people came.

Everyone was uncomfortable. The expectant mother was embarrassed, and the two or three others who came felt bad for her. The two who planned it were angry with all the other gals in the class and church who should have been there but weren't. They would swear that they would never do another shower. They felt like not speaking to all those who didn't show up. It would be weeks before emotions returned to normal.

Later, they learned the secret to a successful shower. Two ladies would get together and make the basic plans. Then they planned an organization for the shower and made assignments. They spread the work load out and involved many other women in putting together the shower. They made assignments like the following:

Two gals were in charge of invitations.

Two more were in charge of phoning to see who was coming.

Three were in charge of decorations.

Three were put in charge of refreshments.

Two were put in charge of shower games.

One was put in charge of recording shower gifts and who gave them so the expectant mother could keep track and send thank-you notes.

Two were put in charge of cleanup.

They learned that if they did this, it was likely that almost fifteen would be at the shower, even if just those who had a job showed up. No one was embarrassed; no one got mad.

We need to apply the "baby shower philosophy" to our programming. Get more people involved. Find jobs to put people to work on that will add to the accomplishing of the goals of your program.

What we are talking about here is delegating. John White, in *Excellence in Leadership*, makes the following comments about delegating.

Leaders' motives must be right. The most common failure is to not delegate, either because the leader suffers from a need to cling to power or else because the leader cannot trust others. The result is that needed tasks never get done. People who could have carried them out grow bored and feel useless. . . .

On the other hand, a leader's motive in making the particular assignment may be to pass unpleasant tasks to others. Fellow workers quickly perceive this and grow resentful. Leaders should be willing to do themselves any task they assign others. Or they should be willing to help those to whom the tasks have been delegated. Good leaders keep a close watch on their fellow workers' needs. Personal power, personal glory, personal ease are never priorities in the minds of good leaders. They are concerned both with the task and the needs of those sharing in it.[1]

Be Flexible

Once you have your job flow chart, be willing to be flexible and adaptable with it. Don't make it a ball and chain. It is to serve you.

Recruit From the Top Down

Once you have made out a job flow chart for a program, avoid the temptation to try and start the ministry yourself. Make sure you recruit the top-level people first, and let them begin the ministry. Let them be involved in the first stages of the planning and carrying out of the details.

Also, when you get to recruiting, be sure and let the program's leaders recruit their own people. Don't you as a leader go and recruit the lower level people and then turn them over to the program leaders. The leaders will feel more responsibility for their program if they are involved in the recruiting, and the people they recruit will be more responsible and faithful to the leaders if they recruited them.

Keep the Cart Behind the Horse

If someone gets all excited about a program or ministry and they want to get it started, stop. First be sure it is something your church or adult ministry can and wants to back. Then make sure you or some other ministry leader sits down with the prospective leader to plan out the basics, including the job flow chart, for the ministry. Then make sure this leader

"Well, we do need volunteers

will go and recruit others who share the same interest and concern for the ministry. If the leader can't recruit a team to work with the ministry, that ministry likely won't get far.

Keep It Manageable

In a job flow chart, the rule of thumb is that there should not be more than six or seven people answering to any one person in the organization. Six or seven are plenty to keep up with and carry out one's mission.

Let Go

You must be willing to trust people and let them try their ministry wings. Use good judgment, but don't demonstrate such a lack of trust that you have to do everything or make all the decisions.

Maintain Accountability

You need to hold people accountable for their jobs. We often feel very uneasy about this in the church; we feel that it isn't our place to correct or guide people when they are volunteers working for the Lord. That is all the more reason we need to provide guidance and correction. Since the work is for the Lord, the results are very important. The best way I know to guide people and to evaluate their performance is through the use of the *Ministry/Project Planner* that you will learn about in chapter 7 of this book.

Beware the "Bonsai Factor"

You must keep in mind that a basic principle of growth for any organization is enlarging the structure of the organization. The organization must continually allow for more people to help in the more significant and important tasks. I call this the "fish factor" or the "bonsai factor."

Years ago, while visiting Big Bear Lake in Southern California, I noticed what seemed to be giant goldfish around the boat dock. I had never seen goldfish so large. The manager of the docks said they were simply little goldfish that families had brought up to the lake and let loose. A small goldfish, given a larger body of water in which to grow, will grow ten to twelve inches long!

The same principle in reverse is illustrated by the bonsai trees. Bonsai trees are trees that are deliberately dwarfed by restricting and pruning the root system. To bonsai a tree, then, is to dwarf it through these cultivation methods. Unfortunately, we bonsai the church or our adult ministries, too, when we fail to enlarge the structure. We restrict the root base by trying to have the same number of people do an ever-increasing number of jobs. They can't keep up with it. They may get burned out. Their effectiveness may get watered down. The ministries don't grow. A variety of factors get blamed for it, but it's often the bonsai factor at work.

The Job Flow Chart

Following are two samples of job flow charts. The first (page 22) is for an adult ministries program of a church. It is brief, showing only the various departments in the program. Each department should be developed completely like the second flow chart (page 23). It is for an adult Sunday school department. (Note that the adult Sunday school department appears on the first flow chart.)

Obviously, the size of your charts will be somewhat different from these, depending on the size of your church and its ability to conduct a variety of ministries. You will need to adapt these charts to make them useful. That will take some time and effort. Experiment with them. Ask some others to give their opinions and advice. But don't ignore them, and don't try to use them simply "as is." We developed these charts for our specific situation, and you will need to develop yours for your specific situation.

Once you have developed your flow charts, you need to make a job description for each position, detailing the duties involved. Keep the job descriptions simple, yet complete.

Notes

[1]White, *Excellence in Leadership*, p. 341.

Flow Chart for Adult Ministries Program

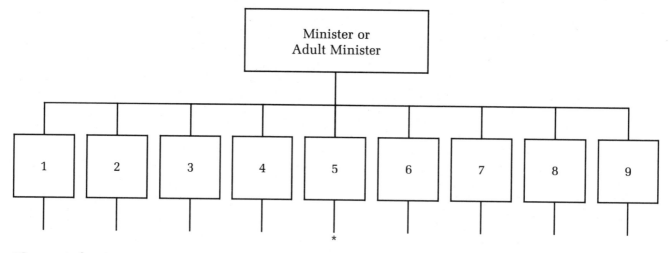

*See next chart.

1 = Records Secretary
2 = Outreach Secretary
3 = Calendar Secretary
4 = Promotions/Advertising Secretary
5 = Adult Sunday School Superintendant (Director)
6 = Men's Ministries Director
7 = Women's Ministries Director
8 = Home Bible Studies Director
9 = Recreation Director

Flow Chart for Adult Sunday School Department

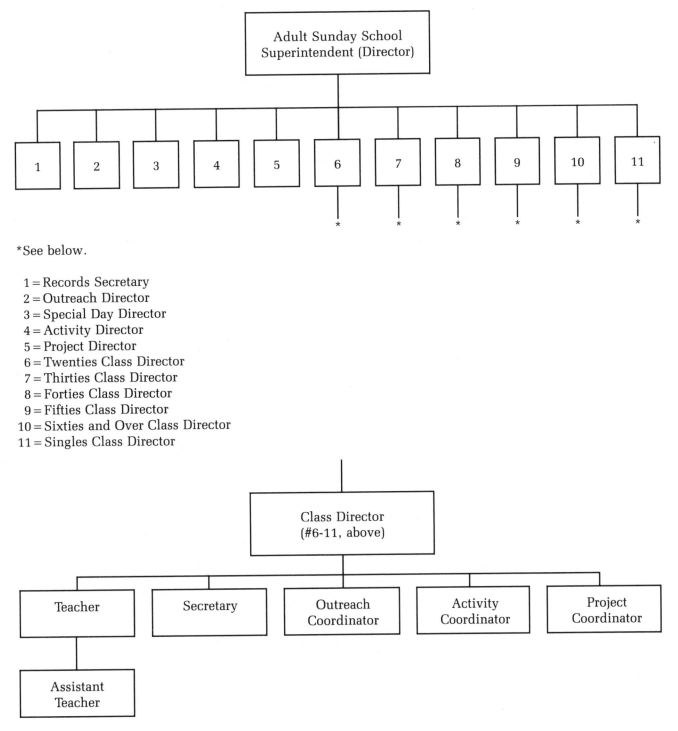

*See below.

1 = Records Secretary
2 = Outreach Director
3 = Special Day Director
4 = Activity Director
5 = Project Director
6 = Twenties Class Director
7 = Thirties Class Director
8 = Forties Class Director
9 = Fifties Class Director
10 = Sixties and Over Class Director
11 = Singles Class Director

Chapter Four

Recruiting People to Adult Ministry

Recruiting is a tough job. It is very time consuming and can be discouraging. The results you get and the frustration you experience will largely be determined by whether or not you accept some basic facts and then develop a good recruiting strategy.

Basic Facts About Recruiting
1. It is hard work.
2. It is time consuming.
3. Not many want to do it.
4. It is a skill that must be learned.
5. You will need to approach many to get a few positive responses.
6. It is a never-ending job.
7. You will be let down many times.
8. You will often be misled.
9. You will sometimes recruit the wrong person for a job and then have to figure out how to undo the damage that person has done and how to get him out of the job without causing more damage.
10. You won't get 100% results. (Remember, however, getting 30% positive responses would make you an all-star in the major leagues.)

Developing a Recruiting Strategy

Being a recruiter for adult ministries in the church demands commitment to the mission. You must be sold on the cause for the Lord and believe in the end goals, or you will throw in the towel and go off and do something you can do all by yourself.

What is recruiting? It is selling people on the mission. It is helping them catch the vision and see the big picture. It is creating a desire on their part to join the ranks and contribute what they have to offer to seeing the mission carried out. It is bartering of the best kind. You are asking a person to give up something he is presently doing in his life (whether it's taking naps, watching T.V., or participating in recreation, family time, reading time, or work time) to invest that time in the cause you have. You must be sold on the mission or you will fail. We live in a day and age when there are a thousand things begging for people's time, attention, and investments. If you are haphazard, sloppy, indifferent, or negative in the way you come across, it would be better to find something else to do. You won't make it. To be a recruiter, you must become a negotiator for the Lord. You are His recruiter—calling people to His ministry.

Recruiting is knowing the mission. It is having a game plan developed enough to present to others and being able to communicate it. Recruiting is showing what will be required of those who join—what it will cost them in time, effort, and money. It is being prepared to show them how you will train and support them, and being able to show them the benefits of the mission and of their involvement in it.

I have found from personal experience that there are several things that don't work in the job of recruiting.
1. Crying—either privately or publicly—as you tell of the need.
2. Crawling to others on your knees.
3. Condemning others for their lack of concern and care.
4. Quitting—or threatening to quit if someone will not help.
5. Ignoring the problem.
6. A constant barrage of clever bulletins, flyers, and announcements.
7. And last but not least—trying to get the preacher to cry, crawl, or condemn everyone not already helping.

What *does* work? How *can* you recruit people? There is no secret formula, no set of magic words. Each recruiter will develop his own style of recruiting. But I believe there are some basics that ought to be followed as one develops his strategy.

Recruiting Basics

Start With Prayer

Prayer must be our starting point. It was for Jesus. He spent an entire night in prayer before He chose twelve of His disciples to be apostles (Luke 6:12, 13). He said, "The harvest is plentiful but the workers are few. Ask the Lord of the harvest, therefore, to send out workers into his harvest field" (Matthew 9:37, 38). So pray. Pray for the ministry, its needs, and its goals. Pray for specific people to become involved. Prayer must be a year-round activity in adult ministry.

Recruit One-on-one

The most effective recruiting is *one-on-one*. It is the only kind of recruiting that will get good results when you are recruiting people to a ministry that is ongoing and takes a commitment from them. There will always be exceptions to this, but don't plan your strategy based on the exceptions. You may get many people to sign up on a registration card to bring cookies, or to house members of a choir passing through town, but you can't count on that as the way to get all the teachers you need for Sunday school or some other ongoing ministry.

Once you know whom you want to recruit, contact that person and set up an appointment, a set time when you can sit down with that person and make your own presentation. It can be in the recruit's home, at church, at a restaurant, or at your own home. But you want the encounter to be face-to-face. The more important the task, the more important that you set up a face-to-face meeting with adequate time to talk.

Doug Osness, Minister of Evangelism at Central, has applied this to his recruiting of Ambassadors for the evangelism program. He has three other men in this recruiting ministry working with him. Their goal is for each of them to make one recruiting call a week. That totals sixteen a month between them. They set up appointments with the people. On the visit, they share what the Ambassador Training is by means of a video presentation and printed materials. They seek to recruit them into the training face-to-face.

Karen Wilson, our Family Circle Leader at Central, began recruiting people to become leaders of these home Bible studies by having them over to her home for dinner. It was much easier to talk to them about becoming involved in the ministry in this friendly setting. She was also communicating to them that she was going to support them and get involved in their lives. She has good results from this face-to-face approach.

Have a Year-round Recruiting Plan

I recommend having a year-round strategy for recruiting. You may have people who need to step out of their ministries at various times during the year; so you will continually need to be filling spots throughout the year. If you are not prepared to fill those spots whenever they become vacant, you will

have to set the ministries they represent aside for a while, which is usually not helpful.

There are a variety of aspects you might want to include in your yearlong plan. I recommend at least the following.

a. Have a *new-member orientation* program or plan. A basic part of such a plan is a class for new members. At Central, we have two. Our "Central Basics" class for new members is a four-week class offered every month on Sunday mornings. Our Discover Victory class is an eight-week class and is also offered on Sunday mornings.

The new members' classes are not the only part of our orientation plan, however. They do not even represent the first step. The first step is a meeting with an orientation representative.

When someone joins the church, an orientation representative immediately makes an appointment to meet with the new member, preferably that same week. When they meet, the following things happen:

1. The orientation representative reaffirms our welcome of the new member into our fellowship.
2. He gives the new member a new member's packet, consisting of a book on Christian growth (*Where Do You Grow From Here?*, by LeRoy Lawson, ©1985 by Standard Publishing), a cassette tape with a welcome message from Dr. Lawson, and an explanation of our Central Basics class and Discover Victory class.
3. The new member is invited to enroll in the new-member classes. It is not important which the new member takes first. If it is time for a new Central Basics class to begin, we encourage the new member to take that first. If not, we try to enroll him in the Discover Victory class. We want all our new members to take both of these classes.
4. Finally, the representative invites the new member to get involved in what we call an entry-level job in the church. This job is very simple, but it gets the person involved.

During the Central Basics class, staff members and program directors each get about ten minutes to explain what ministries they are working with and how people can get involved in these ministries. About half of each session consists of these presentations. We hope that during this first month of their involvement, they will be introduced to a ministry with which they can get involved in a significant way. Many of them do respond to these invitations to serve.

b. We have begun an annual *Ministry Fair*. Each September, when everyone is getting back in the swing of things after summer, we have each ministry area or department in the church set up an attractive

"Just kidding about the trip to Hawaii, folks.
We just needed some volunteers."

PORTLOK

booth in our foyer. We want something of a convention atmosphere. Each department supplies its own booth and the people to mind it. We encourage our people to browse and investigate the booths to learn more about the ministries and to see which one(s) they can get involved in. Sundays during this time are dedicated to preaching about service, ministry, and using our gifts for the Lord. We also have a Saturday training program soon after this emphasis so people recruited during this time can be offered immediate training.

c. I recommend that people in charge of recruiting for a particular ministry have a *recruiting tool*. It may be a box, packet, or envelope with materials, a brochure, or a booklet. Sixteen years ago, when I was working as a youth minister, I prepared such a tool and found it very helpful to me. It was a notebook made up with pictures of youth and adults in a variety of settings to reinforce the theme of the presentation, which was "Twenty Opportunities in Working With Youth." I also had the twenty opportunities printed up on one sheet of paper, and I would leave that with the prospective youth worker. I've had a variety of other items over the years to use in recruiting people. It helps most people to have a tool in hand to use as a guide in their presentation. Just a word of caution. Don't forget the acrostic "K.I.S.S." Keep it simple stupid! Don't make your pack so complicated or huge that it frightens people off.

d. Another method we have used in recruiting people is what we call a *preview party* or session. When we started our Family Circles (our home Bible-study program), we handpicked a number of people we wanted to see become leaders in the Circles and sent them a personalized letter inviting them to a preview meeting. We had a couple of parties so we could keep them small and also offer a couple of options for convenience. Their coming was to help them learn about the program. Coming didn't obligate them to be leaders. It only obligated them to investigate and decide yes or no. We told them the length and nature of the meeting. We had handouts. Refreshments were served. A presentation was made, questions were answered, and then we sent them home to think and pray about it. We followed up within a week by phoning to see what they had decided. If they were interested, we signed them up for the training program. Variations of this have worked in a variety of programs.

Areas of Concern

A genuine frustration that sometimes arises is not being able to find the people or the person you need in order to get a ministry started and/or to keep it going. God's timing plays an important part in our recruiting, and we must be willing to live with that and not fight it. When you are eager to start something that seems needed and obvious, but the leadership isn't present, it is very difficult to wait till the leaders arise.

If you find yourself in that situation, then keep praying and looking, but don't feel guilty because you can't get the program started. Don't resort to doing it yourself unless you free yourself of some other responsibilities. You can only do so many things before you spread yourself out so thin that you become ineffective in all your ministries. Wait on the Lord to help lift up the right people, and start the ministry then.

A major item of concern in recruiting people is trying to match the right people to the ministry. If a person isn't gifted in teaching, you don't want to make him a teacher. The teacher won't like it, the class won't like it, and you won't like the situation you have to deal with. The next chapter deals with the issue of helping people discover their gifts and using them appropriately. Over the years, I have always tried to help people find a ministry they would like to be involved with rather than just use them to fill the holes I needed filled. If you recruit someone to an area for which they are not gifted or that they don't like, most of the time you will soon have to recruit someone for it again. The ungifted person won't function well and/or will quit. Then you'll be back where you started. Recruiting according to gifts and interests complicates the matter because you may have to talk to many more people in recruiting for your ministry needs, but you will be better off in the long run.

When you can't get the needed help for a certain ministry, you have several options. You can wait until you get the help before you continue the ministry. You can simply shut it down. If it is a ministry you feel can't wait or be shut down, you may have to try something extremely innovative—even drastic.

We ran into a difficult situation at Central that illustrates this. When we moved into our new facility in the fall of 1986, we began an accelerated period of growth in the life of the church. From 1985 to 1987, the congregation almost doubled in size. A lot of new people, many with no church background and training came into the church. We had hundreds of little preschool and nursery children and too few helpers. Our preschool people didn't know most of the new people. We tried many ways of getting help, but we continued to have too many kids and not enough help.

A proposal was made and taken to the elders for their support, which they gave. The proposal stated that for a six-month trial period, all members of the church with children of kindergarten-age or less would be expected to help at least once a month somewhere in this department if they wanted their children to attend any of the preschool classes. This was to solve a problem for which we couldn't wait a year for a solution. We expected some parents would not like it, but we concluded that if parents wouldn't help with the spiritual care and development of their own kids, we would be in trouble in the long run. Non-parents were helping, and still do help, in this area, but this was a way we had to deal with one department that needed a huge number of workers in a short amount of time. The parents were the logical ones to help meet the need.

Before this proposal was ever formally announced or implemented, one of our creative preschool department coordinators found a way to get all the help she needed for her area. She wrote a letter to all the members of the church who were parents of children in her area. It was a nice letter, simply explaining the need for help in that ministry area. She drew up a chart assigning each of those parents to help one Sunday in the following couple of months. She didn't ask them; she just assigned them a time and said in her letter that if they had a conflict, they should let her know so another time could be arranged. She also included a brief explanation of what they would be doing when they helped.

Her plan ws successful. The parents showed up, and she got the help she needed. These parents were helpers, not teachers. But once they get involved, people begin to show more interest, and many of these parents will become regular workers, and some of them will become teachers.

A lot more was involved in this effort than I will share here. This simply shows that sometimes, in some situations, you have to use a very innovative plan to get critically needed help. I wouldn't recommend you do this very often or in very many areas, but sometimes you simply do what you have to do.

How Do You Find the People to Recruit?

Figuring out whom to recruit to fill your ministry needs can be perplexing. It demands regular attention. You almost need to become a headhunter for the Lord; not in the sense of stealing people from other ministries, but as one always on the search for people to recruit. Jesus did that. I get the feeling He walked through the crowds looking for people who would be willing to become His followers and "fishers of men." So where do you find recruits for your ministry needs?

Keep Your Eyes Open

For a leader in charge of recruiting people, it is good advice to walk slowly through the crowds with an eye open for people to talk to about involvement in the ministry. You will normally be attending activities sponsored by your church, from the regular services to fellowship dinners and receptions. You must become a meeter and greeter of people. Take the initiative. Introduce yourself to people you don't

know. Get to know them. Ask them about their families, their occupations, and special interests or hobbies. Ask them about their Christian background and experience. As you get to know people, you will become better at recruiting them. You must take the initiative in this whole process. Don't wait for people to come running to you, eager to help.

Get Involved

It is easier and more natural to recruit people you know. It will be helpful, then, if you can become involved with a group of potential recruits in the church.

At another church several years ago, I started a young couples Sunday-school class. The class grew to average forty or fifty each week. I did most of my visitation on prospects for that class, I counseled many of them, we went on canoe trips together; we were together a lot! I was also in charge of the total Sunday-school program. What I found out after a

"We're in need of a volunteer."

while was that the class wouldn't grow beyond forty or fifty because I kept recruiting people out of there to teach in other areas of the Sunday-school program. It was natural. Here at Central, I saw the same thing happen with Steve Palich, our adult education director. He also leads the singles ministry. As that group has grown and he spends time with them, he is heavily recruiting and involving the singles in all sorts of ministries.

One person can't be involved in all the various areas of adult life in the church. You might not even be able to get heavily involved with any one group. In that case, find some active people in every major area and make them your recruiters in each area. They know the people. They spend time with them. You recruit and train the recruiters and send them out to recruit from the crowds with which they spend their time. Develop them into a team. You will need to meet with them and keep them excited about their recruiting ministry, but it will be time well spent.

Live With the Rolodex™

Nothing has proven more helpful over the years in finding names of people to recruit than regularly going through the Rolodex™ (which contains the church membership list) and writing down names of people I would like to recruit. Many of them I knew; others were strangers to me. I have often sat down with others in the office and gone over the names and asked them for information on the people I did not know well. As I have regularly gone over the membership list, I have discovered that nearly every time, I catch a name that I missed all the other times I had gone through it. Sometimes this process leads me to reconsider someone I had intentionally gone over before. Sometimes my reasons for passing over them weren't very good, or the situation has changed since then.

Approach Groups to Help

There are occasions when your recruitment needs can be met by going to a specific group and either asking for individuals from the group to help with a project or for the entire group to take it on. There have been a number of ministries in the adult area that we have asked groups to perform. Our senior adults, our singles, our women's groups, our men's fellowship, and our college-age group have all taken on specific projects and given good results.

Involve New Members and Non-members Who Attend Regularly

Develop a system to make sure that you approach all your new members to get them involved in a ministry. I have already explained how we do it at Central. You may want to copy that plan or develop your own, but do not ignore this potential group of workers. It's good for your program and for them to get them involved early in ministry. A word of caution, here. You need to be sure you are aware of your congregation's requirements for people who serve in different areas. In our congregation, a person must be a member in order to teach in Sunday school. There are, however, many jobs and ministries that non-members (regular attenders who are not members) can be involved in. Make sure you are aware of your church's policy so you may abide by it.

Some Observations About Recruiting

If you can recruit ten people to give four hours a week, you have just recruited the equivalent of one full-time staff person.

Sometimes, those who work with volunteers think, "If I could only pay people for the jobs I need help with, it would solve all my recruiting problems." This is sometimes true, but more often than not it is an illusion. Most people can be motivated by things other than money.

Recruiting takes good promotion. You need to keep the needs before the people in a variety of different and creative ways. Beat the drum and send out the message. The best recruitment is still one-on-one, but you need to get their attention in a variety of ways. Keep the need before them.

The issue of asking people for a designated length of time or service commitment has been argued back and forth. I recommend asking people to make a one-year commitment to serving in the ministry they accept with the option of making a change at the end of the year. Those who are most often opposed to doing this suggest that people ought to be willing to serve for twenty years, or forty, if they are gifted in particular areas and as long as there is a need. To have one-year terms of service doesn't negate long-term commitment, nor does it suggest that everyone and anyone should bounce around every year from one ministry to another. Most won't.

I first used the one-year commitment several years ago. I had several fears when I started doing it. I was most fearful that at the end of the year, seventy-five percent or more of my teachers would want to quit. My fears were happily proven wrong. Few did.

Let me share the advantages I have found by asking my entire staff to sign up for one year at a time in their ministries.

First, it puts recruiting on a schedule. You have a yearlong agenda to work with. This could even be tied in with a ministry recruitment month and fair that would precede your training events.

When working on a one-year sign-up basis, you need to figure out your calendar year. Let's say you decide on June through May. In February, you would want to survey your current workers and see who will "re-up" for the next year. Then you will know how many replacements you need and in what areas. Then you need to decide what new classes or groups you want to start for the next ministry year. From those two factors you can decide how many workers you need to recruit and train.

Then in March you can run your recruiting emphasis and programs. In April, you would offer your major training events. In May, you would assign people to their ministries and help them get settled. They would actually start serving in June. This gives them the summer to get settled and adjust to their new ministry before school starts back up.

Second, it allows you to concentrate your recruiting efforts. You will still need to be recruiting during the entire year, but the big push, the major time of pressure is condensed. Recruiting is hard work, as I have already said. It drains you. It is easier to deal with the pressure in a major way for three or four months than having the cloud hang over you for twelve months.

Third, people tend to keep their commitments. Some will still need to quit during the year, but the number is greatly reduced. Most people will at least serve out their year.

Fourth, you can tie your recruiting in with your major training programs for the year. You are recruiting people to be trained. Most churches can't offer training every month of the year. This allows you to have the training when you bring in the largest number of recruits ready for it.

Fifth, it allows you to give people an "honorable" way to switch ministries, take time off, or step out of the ministry they are in. Often, when people accept a ministry in the church, they are still seeking to find their gifts and their areas of service for the Lord. People's desires and interests change over the years, too. I would rather have a person serving in an area where he is gifted than to be in a spot where he feels stuck. When people get in the wrong ministry, it can be very hard to get out. They can feel, or be made to feel, like they are letting down the Lord, the church, and the U.S. Congress if they quit! This gives people a way to move gracefully.

Finally, this gives you, the leader, an opportunity to do a simple evaluation with all your volunteer workers. You can make up an evaluation form to meet your needs. It can simply consist of asking the workers to do a self-examination of the past year's ministry. What went well? Where can they improve? You can use this as a time to praise them as well as to make suggestions for growth and improvement. This will be helpful and must be done without harshness or a condemning spirit.

Helping People Find Their Gifts for Ministry

A very rewarding part of ministry in the church is helping people find their gifts for ministry. It is like shell hunting on the beach. The excitement is picking them up to see whether you have discovered something of uniqueness and beauty. You never know what you will find. There are some people in the church who seem to know their gifts early in their Christian lives and there never seems to be any question. I believe most Christians never really discover what their gifts are, however. Thus, they never develop those gifts. Part of recruiting, training, and developing adult workers is helping adults find and develop their ministries. It is hard to recruit people to do something they are not skilled or gifted in. So part of your strategy in adult ministry is helping those who don't know what their gifts are to find them and then to motivate those people to use and develop their newfound gifts.

This is the basic philosophy I have worked with over the years. I have tried to help people find where their gifts and skills are and put them to work in those areas. I have tried to start with "Where would you like to serve the Lord?" I would rather have a person serving in an area where he feels comfortable and gifted than simply filling a hole I needed filled in the ministry. It can create a lot of problems when you get people in the wrong areas either by railroading them or by exploiting their willingness to be of help. Such people are generally not as motivated for the tasks, their preparation is not as thorough, and their attitude may not be very good. Besides that, they may simply not be very good at their assigned tasks. That is not their fault. They are just in the wrong places. They would probably be very good at some other tasks. The job of Christian leaders is to help each person find his spot—his place of service.

When you have someone in the wrong area, you have four alternatives. First, you may be able to leave the person in that ministry role, but train him to serve well. Many people are trainable and easily learn to do new things. Second, you may be able to transfer the worker to another ministry where he can serve well. A third alternative is to ask the worker to step aside. This must be done gently and with love, and can cause a number of problems. We often are afraid of hurting people's feelings and, thus, we shy away from this option. But in the long run, it may be preferable to the fourth option, which is to ignore the problem and leave the ineffective worker in his position without training. This is the worst choice, but it's very common.

Another matter of importance in helping people serve in the areas where they are gifted has to do with the "fruit of the Spirit" (Galatians 5:22). Demonstrating the fruit of the Spirit in one's life is more important than the gifts the person has. The New Testament gives several examples of people who had gifts or abilities, but did not demonstrate the fruit of the Spirit. Such people will do more harm than good.

This principle does suggest that it is wise to select leaders who have both relational and functional skills for a program the congregation has decided to make one of its major offerings. Regrettably, a vast number of churches select program leaders on the basis of just the functional competencies they bring to their positions. Insufficient attention is given to whether or not the leaders of the program have strong relational competencies as well.[1]

Helping people find their gifts for ministry can be an outcome of your contact with people and getting to know them better. As you spend time with people, notice how well they get along with other people. Notice what types of ministry activities they do best and what ideas and ministry possibilities excite them. Keep your eyes open to notice peoples' gifts. You may be pleasantly surprised.

We currently have some staff members at Central who were working in other occupations and careers not so long ago. They were members here and volunteered for ministries that matched their gifts. They did such an outstanding job that, when it was time to hire staff members in those areas of ministry, it was

"He said the V word."

obvious to us that they were the people we wanted. That wouldn't have happened if they had been involved in ministries where they were not gifted.

When you see someone with undeveloped or unused skills or gifts for the Lord, talk to that person. See whether you can find a ministry where those gifts would be valuable. You may even need to start a new ministry to put that person to work. Do it. When you match a person's gifts to ministry, watch out! Some great things can happen.

Besides noticing gifts as you observe people in your current program, you should have a program that is designed to help people find their gifts. I have already explained our program for doing that with new members. Basically it involves a meeting with an orientation representative, the four-week Central Basics class, and the eight-week Discover Victory class.

It is vitally important to get new members involved in ministry when possible. The writers of *A Passion for Excellence* make some interesting comments about bringing new people into businesses. We can learn something from them about incorporating new people into our churches and ministries.

Educating well ("overeducating" by most of the world's standards) at the beginning—bringing newcomers into the organization and making them a part of it in a short time—is the bedrock of sustained creative contributions. Educating is not about giving instructions. It's acting on a deep-down belief in the potential of every person to contribute, over time, by providing the tools, the elbowroom and frequent, concrete, believable feedback about progress.[2]

Some churches are too slow in bringing newcomers into their organization and making them a part of it in a short time. I'm not suggesting you make new members elders after two months, but you can get people involved in many ministries. If they prove unfaithful or unreliable, then deal with that. But don't wait two years to involve people. You will lose most of them in that time.

Another way you can program to help people find their gift of ministry if by offering classes, seminars, and preaching series. In our Center for Biblical Service program, we offer a class on finding one's gift. We use Knofel Station's manual titled *Discovering My Gifts for Service* for the class. His book is published by Standard Publishing and is a good group study in helping people share together as they seek and search how they can best serve the Lord.

Notes

[1]Callahan, *Twelve Keys*, p. 66.

[2]Peters, Austin, *Passion for Excellence*, p. 341.

Chapter Five

Training People for Adult Ministry

With but a few exceptions, it is cruel and unusual punishment to recruit a person to a ministry (even if it is a ministry that the person is gifted for) and put him into it without offering training first or very early in that person's service. To teach a Sunday-school class or a home Bible study, to lead and serve in services, to call in the hospital, or to serve in any way, people deserve the privilege of being trained. Training people for ministry is a vital and demanding step, but it is often neglected or over-looked.

A professional football team spends thousands of hours and millions of dollars on training. It has rookie camps for the new guys on the block. They come out and begin learning the team's system and getting familiar with life in the pros. Then comes the pre-season camp, when the rookies and the veterans join ranks and continue conditioning and trying out for various position. It's the time when the coaches begin making the decisions as to who is best at each spot, and they work with the players in helping them develop their skills. Then, during the season, the coaches meet together for hundreds of hours planning their workouts. They hold "skull sessions" (talking, thinking, and planning) with the team, helping the players get ready for the next game. All this energy and work goes into getting ready to play sixty minutes of football.

How can we not give training a high priority in our work in the church? How can we expect to have people get excited about ministry if we don't prepare them and equip them? What player would get excited about playing in the NFL if he showed up at pre-season camp and they never had meetings, workouts, or training, and they only handed out half the equipment the players needed to wear? How well would that team do during the season if that continued?

Concepts in Training Your Recruited Adult Workers

Yearlong Strategy

You must have a yearlong strategy for training your people. A football team has a year-round plan for recruiting and training, and the church needs one, too.

You need "rookie camps" or initial training sessions. You need to offer training for those who are new to your church or to the ministry they are beginning. You don't need to make your experienced teachers take it again, but you do need to have an entry-level training program for every ministry to which you recruit.

Then you need "pre-season camp" training. Those who are experienced need to be growing in their skills and abilities for their ministries. Some elements in this training will be too advanced for rookies, but your veterans need them to keep them growing.

Last you need "skull-session" training. This is the ongoing times of getting together for sharing, training, brainstorming, revising, and getting ready for the next "game" or session or lesson. The leaders of a ministry ought to have regular staff meetings. Just because you are working with volunteers doesn't mean you don't need to keep in touch and work together. Our adult Sunday-school teachers meet together weekly. Our home Bible-study leaders meet together every Sunday night. You have to determine how often skull sessions are needed for the leaders of your ministry for them to function efficiently.

Regular teachers'/leaders' meetings are a must in order to have efficient year-round training of your people. No one needs unnecessary meetings to attend, but holding regular meetings for leaders in a ministry is a major way to continue ongoing training. If you have a monthly meeting with the leaders of a ministry and you spend thirty minutes of each meeting in training, you have added six hours a year to your training strategy. For someone to complain about these meetings and having to attend them might be normal, but not to attend them would make as much sense as a football player not going to the huddles in a game because they bored him, and he didn't like them, and he thought they were a waste of time. You need to make these sessions as interesting, helpful, and motivating as possible. You need to decide how often the leaders of your ministry need to be together in order to do their best at what they are being asked to do.

Variety

Training sessions need to be offered at various times of the year and made available in a variety of ways to reach the most people. Over the past several years, I have concluded that the shorter the rookie-level training sessions are, the greater the participation and the better people stick with it. Friday-night and Saturday-morning sessions are often the best. Four- to seven-week-long sessions can work well. There are exceptions, but I have observed that when we stretch training sessions out to thirteen weeks or longer, we generally start losing a large percentage of those we are trying to train. You can offer training sessions during the Sunday-school hour, Sunday evening before services, and during the week. There have been times when I have held the same training back to back during a month so people who couldn't make one session had an alternative. You must make it convenient for people to get the help you want to offer to them.

Mandatory Training

Training should not be optional for the recruit. In fact, it is better to have the ministry itself optional after training. We have often invited people who were thinking about serving to attend training sessions so that, after the sessions, they could make up their mind whether that ministry was what they wanted to be involved in or not. That option sometimes helps recruit people. Coming to the training does not commit them to serve in a ministry. It simply commits them to consider it. Coming doesn't commit them to start the next day in the ministry, but anyone who commits to serving in the stated area must take the training, period.

Some people may be able to start in a ministry before a training session, and that may be necessary in the case of replacing a worker in an existing ministry. But it must be understood that to continue, the new worker must take the training the first opportunity it is offered. We often are too timid about making such requirements for workers in the church, but we ought not to be. This is the Lord's work. We ought to do it the best we can. If someone doesn't want to be a part of the team and do their preparation and homework, that person should not be asked to serve. Our fear might be that if we start putting standards and expectations upon the people, they will back out. People who want to do a good job seldom back out. They see the value of such requirements. They know the program will benefit from having all the workers trained, not just the ones who take the initiative on their own to participate in it.

Train for Your Specific Curriculum

The next important point about training people is to train them how to use the materials or curriculum you expect them to use. Don't teach them just the basic/general principles on how to teach adults in Sunday school and then hand them their teachers manuals and tell them to go teach. Be sure you teach them how to use the methods and style your curriculum uses. It is easier for the trainees to understand what they are doing then, and it helps build confidence in the materials you are giving them. It also builds confidence in themselves. They don't have to go home after the training and try and interpret how to use and apply what you taught them to the new and unfamiliar materials.

Another concept that can help in recruiting and training teachers/leaders is to use the same curriculum across the board in a program whenever possible. There are always those who want to do their own thing and I can understand that, but when trying to run a program, it really is much easier to have all the units doing the same. At Central, our adult Sunday-school classes all study the same thing at the same time. They are on the same study schedule. Our home Bible study groups are all on the same curriculum. In our evangelism program, the *Ambassadors for Christ* training program, published by Standard Publishing, we teach our evangelists (Ambassadors) all how to teach the same three lessons to prospects (*A Peace Treaty With God*). The advantages of doing this are as follows:

1. The church is studying together. There is some harmony in the direction the congregation is going.

2. It makes it easier for the preacher to decide his preaching schedule. He doesn't start preaching on a subject some class just decided to study also.

3. It makes it much easier to introduce inexperienced teachers into Sunday school or some other teaching program. You can have a meeting with all the teachers at the same time and work with them on the same lessons rather than having to work with several different curricula. You probably have time for one regular meeting, but not for getting together to help several new teachers learn to use different curricula.

4. Experienced teachers can help the new teachers learn how to teach, solve problems, or get ideas on how to teach a lesson.

5. It's more convenient to arrange for substitute teachers when all classes are on the same curriculum. You can have a few people always prepared to substitute who can step into any class and teach if

they have the same material. If every class is doing something different, it greatly complicates the whole process.

Training Programs and Leaders

Church staff members don't have to do all the training. Allow *members of the congregation* to use their skills, and give them the opportunity to develop the skills to train others. This can become a strong motivating factor in their life in the church. There are many people in most congregations who can be used in training programs. They may need to be trained to do so, but why not? Expand their ministries. Let them have a bigger vision of how God can use them in His work.

Don't be afraid to use *people from other churches* to help you in your training. There may be people in other churches who have expertise in a ministry that no one in your church does. Don't be afraid to use them. You probably would want to meet with them and go over how they could help and what they would do. You might also suggest to one or two of your people that they attend the training with an outside consultant so that they can become the trainers for your church in the future.

Another possibility in training is to *work with other churches* in your area and plan a training conference together. I know of several areas where the churches have done this and have an annual Friday-Saturday training program. They can plan it together with their churches' needs in mind and then pool their trainers to offer better training than any one of them might be able to offer alone.

An obvious way to train your people is to take advantage of all the local, state and national *training conferences, conventions, and seminars* held by publishers, churches, individuals, denominations, and colleges. Some of the best training available can be found at these events.

Another method of training is to develop *self-study programs*. You may have people who will never be able to attend some of your formal training programs because of travel or work schedules, but they are willing to be trained. Or you might recruit someone or have someone offer to help months before you are able to offer rookie-level training again. Rather than put these people on hold, you could develop a training program they could take home and use. With the training materials you use in your regular training programs, you could set up a

"We told them if they came to the Volunteer Seminar there would be doughnuts and coffee. They came, they ate, and they left!"

self-guided outline of reading and worksheets. In our day and age, with easy access to videos, you could make your own training videos. Tape your regular training sessions and use them. You've got to use all the methods available to get the job done!

Use *professionally developed training programs* that you can purchase, or rent. Most major Christian publishing houses have a variety of training programs and resources which you need to examine. Find the ones that best suit you needs and goals. Don't waste your time re-inventing the wheel when others already have good materials available. Standard Publishing, for example, has published the following resources available which would be excellent to use in training adults for adult ministries.

1. *Training Successful Teachers* (#18-03204). This kit includes a leader's guide, training manuals for four different age groups, visuals, a filmstrip, and other resources.

2. *You Can Teach Successfully* series. These are the training manuals from the kit above, and are also available individually.
   You Can Teach Preschoolers Successfully, Betty Aldridge (#18-03205).
   You Can Teach Children Successfully, Twila Sias (#18-03206).
   You Can Teach Teens Successfully, Roy Reiswig (#18-03207).
   You Can Teach Adults Successfully, Ron Davis, Mark Plunkett, Dan Schanz, Rick Shonkwiler, Mark Taylor (#18-03208).

3. *Teach With Success*, Guy Leavitt, revised by Eleanor Daniel (#18-03232).

4. *Basic Principles of Effective Teaching*, June Crabtree (#14-03653).

5. *Training for Service*, Orrin Root, revised by Eleanor Daniel. This includes an instructor's manual (#18-03211), a student manual (#18-03212), and a teaching visuals/resources packet (#18-03213).

6. *New Training for Service*, C. J. Sharp (#18-03059).

7. *Ambassadors for Christ: Training for Evangelism* (#30-03225). This training kit includes everything needed to set up a program to train people to make evangelistic calls. The items, listed below, are also available individually.
   Trainer's Manual (#30-03221). The kit includes one.
   Student's Manual (#30-03222). The kit includes ten.
   A Peace Treaty With God (#30-03223). The kit includes twenty-five.
   Presenting "A Peace Treaty With God" cassette tapes (#30-03224). The kit includes one set (three tapes).
   There is also an "introductory kit" available (#30-03231), which contains one each of the above items.

8. *Recruiting, Training, and Developing Volunteer Youth Workers*, David Roadcup (#18-88590).

9. *Successful Single Adult Ministries*, Krista S. Welsh (#18-03219).

10. *The ABC's of VBS*, Eleanor Daniel (#18-03201).

11. *77 Dynamic Ideas for the Christian Education of the Handicapped*, Jim Pierson (#7970).

Chapter Six

Supporting and Developing People in Adult Ministry

Paul referred to those who worked in the church with him as his partners. I like that word. It pictures people working side by side, seeking to accomplish common goals with more concern about achieving the goals than about rank, status, power, or honor. We have a responsibility to those we recruit and train, our partners. It is to support them or prop them up in their work and ministry. This chapter illustrates some of the different ways you can develop or support your partners in ministry. Remember: these people are your staff. Some may be paid. Most are volunteers. Treat them as what they are; your staff. Do the best you can for them. They deserve it.

Treat people as adults. Treat them as partners; treat them with dignity; treat them with respect.... In A BUSINESS AND ITS BELIEFS, Thomas J. Watson, Jr., puts it well: "IBM's philosophy is largely contained in three simple beliefs. I want to begin with what I think is the most important: our respect for the individual. This is a simple concept, but in IBM it occupies a major portion of management time. We devote more effort to it than anything else."[1]

We must devote a major portion of our management time in the church to people. We exist for people. We must not let our jobs, programs, or papers get in the way of our responsibility toward our people, our partners. We must be committed to them as part of our commitment to the cause of the Lord.

As our workers grow spiritually, the church will benefit. If they fill ministry positions but aren't growing spiritually, those ministries will suffer the consequences. We know we can't force growth on people or manipulate them into growth, but we can do some things to encourage their development.

The purpose of this chapter is to give attention to what we can do for our partners to help them grow. Once you have recruited and trained your partners, your work has just begun. Then the challenge of supporting them in their work begins. Callahan made this great statement:

People are not simply searching for contracts; they are searching for covenant. They are not searching for programs and activities or institutional structures, but for proleptic experiences of kingdom and events of mission in which they can share. They are not searching for a merry-go-round of business activities and committee meetings; they are searching for people with whom they can live out life together.[2]

We ought to help provide this for our partners! Following are some ways you can support your partners in their ministries, and help them experience what Callahan talked about.

Prayer

Let's start with prayer. We prayed to the Lord to lift up workers for the harvest. Now let's continue to keep them in our prayers. Note how often Paul prayed for his partners:

In all my prayers for all of you, I always pray with joy because of your partnership in the gospel from the first day until now (Philippians 1:4, 5).

And this is my prayer: that your love may abound more and more in knowledge and depth of insight, so that you may be able to discern what is best and may be pure and blameless until the day of Christ, filled with the fruit of righteousness that comes through Jesus Christ—to the glory and praise of God (Philippians 1:9-11).

And we pray . . . that you may live a life worthy of the Lord and may please him in every way: bearing fruit in every good work, growing in the knowledge of God, being strengthened with all power according to his glorious might so that you may have great endurance and patience, and joyfully giving thanks to the Father (Colossians 1:10-12).

We continually remember before our God and Father your work produced by faith, your labor prompted by love, and your endurance inspired by hope in our Lord Jesus Christ (1 Thessalonians 1:3).

Our desire for our partners (those we recruit and train) is the same as Paul's for his partners. We want to see them mature and grow in Christlikeness. The stronger they are spiritually, the more fruitful their service to the Lord will be. You might want to adopt Paul's prayers and use them for your own partners.

It doesn't seem too much to suggest that those we want to see grow in the Lord be on our daily prayer list. It doesn't take much time to pray for your people every day. Start a prayer list and begin lifting these people before the Lord.

Pray *with* them, at times. We can get into the same trap as individuals that we can as a group. We can get so busy—even busy in God's work—that we run out of time to pray to the one we are serving. As a group, we can get so busy doing things that we don't make time to pray together. We have times when our staff meets to do nothing but pray. We occasionally vary the times we meet and the frequency of our meetings, but we know we need to pray together. Your staff, whether volunteer or paid, needs the same. Rosalind Rinker came out with some books some time back on conversational prayer. If you haven't experienced conversational prayer, I would suggest you get one of your books and read it. It will show you how to lead your partners in meaningful prayer together. Then do it. Monthly, weekly, or whatever—spend some periods of time together in prayer.

Your Example

You also support your partners by being an example to them of how to work. A leader isn't one who plans the work and dumps it all on others to do. Your partners need to see you working with them. John White made an interesting observation of Nehemiah:

Nehemiah is not the type of leader who avoids sweating. For him leadership is not status, exempting him from common tasks to concentrate on more "important" work. In his first address to Jerusalem Jews he cries, "Let us start rebuilding" (2:18). The words are significant. The *us* is not a rhetorical device. It becomes clear in chapter 4 that he joined in the physical work and the physical hardships. . . . Nehemiah shared hardship with the workers. His beard would be clogged with grit, his eyes red with dust while sweat would probably leave streaks down his cheeks.

Spirituality is no substitute for sweat. Nehemiah's organizing ability, his coolness under stress and his prayers would have been wasted had he not worked. Prayer may move mountains. But prayer and elbow grease are wonderful allies. They make projects hum.[3]

Meetings

Meetings are also important. We all know meetings can be boring, but that doesn't do away with the need for them. We can work at making them productive. To fail to have meetings with your staff would be like a football team never having a huddle to call their next play. You might be able to call a couple plays in one huddle, but not the whole game. Meetings can become the arena for face-to-face communication, and that communication is the basis for involving people and generating enthusiasm.

You can improve the quality of meetings by always working with a printed agenda and a set time limit. I remember attending a meeting with Woody Phillips a few years back. He turned his meeting into a time of worship. He began the meeting with singing some choruses and then had a praise time of prayer. This helped remind everyone as to the nature of the meeting. It was to get the Lord's work done. He was there in their midst. We need to be conscious of that fact in all our meetings.

Meetings can be for communication, training, answering questions, and providing regular support. People don't like unnecessary meetings, but neither do they like not knowing what is going on, or not having a time to communicate with their leaders and co-workers. Our Family Circle leaders meet every Sunday night. Our youth sponsors meet weekly to plan their work. They need to feel they are a team in order to be successful in their work with the kids.

The quality of your ministry can be affected by the frequency and quality of your meetings. Your staff may need to meet weekly, monthly, or quarterly. Be flexible. Our paid staff started out with weekly meetings, but we found out we can do our work meeting every other week. I started meeting with each of the staff members I was supervising weekly. I found later we could get our work done meeting every other week. You have to determine what you need done and then not waste time doing it.

Walking the Floor

A major way you show support for your partners is to do what the business world calls "walking the floor." This means getting out to where your workers are doing their ministry. A great way to lose credibility is never to walk into your partners' classrooms or meetings. You may think you will put them on edge if you do. Actually, you will show them you don't care and you have abandoned them if you don't. You may fear walking into a poorly-run situation, or having to give help, or ending up in the midst of discouraged, frustrated workers who are understaffed and underequipped, and they might tell you they want to quit. If you avoid walking the floor for any of those reasons and you don't get in the midst of what is going on, your partners probably should quit!

Walk the floor. It will help you see how you can help them, and it will give them moral support.

Mail

You can support your partners through the mail in a variety of ways. You can have department newsletters and mailings. We have made up two different kinds of thank-you notes we use with those we are working with. When someone is doing a good job, we can fill out one of the notes and mail it to them. People like being appreciated and a note in the mail shows you are aware of their work. It can be very encouraging to them. About every other month, I like to write a note to my people and simply tell them how much I appreciate them and what they are doing for the Lord. You can also send birthday cards, anniversary cards, and other occasion cards. This takes a little time and a little money, but it shows them they are more than plugs in the holes of your program. They are people who are loved and appreciated.

Recognition and Rewards

The next area deals with recognizing and rewarding your partners for their service. In the business world today, some are calling it "hoopla." Some feel that personal recognition is inappropriate in the church. People are, or ought to be, serving the Lord in love and not for recognition. That is obvious. But that doesn't make it wrong or inappropriate to honor faithful servants. Paul was quick to do so with Timothy and many others, especially in the closing of his letter to the Romans. After acknowledging the service of some men from Corinth, he made the following comment: "Such men deserve recognition" (1 Corinthians 16:18).

"Harold, the pastor says if you don't want to be a volunteer, you don't have to."

How can you recognize your partners? Let me count the ways. You can have *Worker-of-the-Month columns* in your church or department newsletter. You can have a special *bulletin board* with information on your partners. You can have *special awards, plaques, trophies, or certificates* to hand out to your people for a job well done. You can have work or service *anniversary certificates* for the number of years they have been serving in their ministry areas. Be creative and add your own items to the list. Toot their horns before others. They won't.

You can have an annual *appreciation banquet* for all your partners. We host one each fall. Our workers and their mates are our guests. We present all of them with a "Servants Heart" award. Then out of every department, we honor two people with the "Second Mile" award for service above and beyond the call of duty for that year. It is a special night of showing appreciation and giving recognition to those who deserve it.

Getting Away

Taking your people on a retreat or to a conference can be a meaningful way to support them. An annual retreat for fellowship, training, and inspiration is a good way to get your workers ready for fall and winter or to prepare to go into summer. There are normally many different kinds of seminars and conferences offered throughout the year in most larger cities. It can be a boost to your people to take them to one.

It would be a mistake to overlook having time to play or relax with your staff of workers or partners. Spending play time together helps you get to know the whole person. This isn't a major part of our time together by any means, but it helps build our culture. Most of our partners don't become best friends and do everything together away from church, but we are certainly friends and partners in the work of the Lord. We have had some memorable experiences over the years from our play times. We have gone on a few canoe trips together. On our retreats, we have gone on hikes, played volleyball, and sat up late at night playing trivia games. We have had a couple of water skiing days together. Some of our groups of partners from different ministries have gone to music events, sporting events, and had potlucks and parties together. We aren't able to do as much of this as we would like to—we are not here just for us. We are here to work together to reach out. If we spent too much time together having fun and fellowship, all the world would go to Hell. But we plan for some of these events during the year because we believe it is important.

Spiritual Development

Another way to help your partners grow spiritually would be to form "Spiritual T.E.A.M.s" among them. I wrote a discipleship program for Standard Publishing titled *Discipling New Christians With the Spiritual T.E.A.M.* It is a plan designed to get people—especially new Christians—involved in spiritual calisthenics (devotions) time. Two to five or six can make up a T.E.A.M., which meets together once a week. At the T.E.A.M. meeting, members share what they learned in their private study. The first half of the program is thirteen weeks long and is called the Rookie Season. At the conclusion of this, everyone decides whether they would like to go through the second thirteen weeks of the program, called the Veteran Season. This is an excellent way to help your people give attention to their own growth, and to spend time in prayer with them. This could be used to begin an ongoing Bible study for your workers.

Of course, there are many other programs you could use to aid in the spiritual development of your partners. Whether you use the Spitiual T.E.A.M. approach or some other, assisting your workers in developing regular times of study and personal devotions is important. Whatever encouragement you can offer will be valuable.

Reviews and Evaluations

An important way to support and develop your partners is to have a regular plan to review their work and ministry. The idea of a review is frightening to many, but it need not be. In fact, most people really do want to know whether they are doing well at their jobs. They want to know how to improve. If we handle the review process properly, it can be a very beneficial time.

Our hesitation about reviewing the work of our workers often centers on the fact that they are volunteers, not paid workers. We insist on accountability from our paid staff, but we feel it is out of place for volunteers. "After all," we say, "these people are working for God, not me. Who am I to review their work?" But if you are the one who recruited them to the ministry, you are the one to whom they will look for help and direction. You are the one God is using to assist these people in ministry. Thus, you have an obligation to know what the workers are doing and how you can assist them. That can only be accomplished through regular times of review. If this purpose is kept in mind, and if you approach the review with love and compassion, it will be a very profitable experience for you, them, and the church.

There are a few principles you need to keep in mind when planning work reviews:

1. Make sure you have the backing of the church leadership before you begin a major review program.
2. Make sure the purpose of the review is clear. Your first job is to be your partners' biggest fan. You are to support and defend them from all attackers. (Make sure you are not an attacker.) Make the review a major time to praise for jobs well done. The secondary purpose of the review is to determine how to improve your ministries.
3. Be consistent throughout your whole department. You may have different issues to deal with for different positions, but you can't just review a part of your staff.
4. Keep it simple. You don't need to drag out a review by discussing one hundred different points.
5. You must have job descriptions for anyone being reviewed. The job description and any set goals will be the major items for review.
6. Have a set time of the year when reviews will be done. If you work with annual commitments to a ministry, review the ministries at the conclusion of the year before the next year begins.

There are a couple of ways you can review your partners' work. The first is to create an evaluation form and then have each person fill one out and simply share it with you. Most people will tend to be harder on themselves than you will be. You can use this time as a major opportunity to praise the workers for the fine things they are doing. The odds are, they will bring up most of their weak areas. When they do, ask them if they have any plan or ideas on how to grow in those areas. If there are some items they overlooked in the review, you can bring them up at the conclusion by saying something like, "You have a good understanding of how you are doing in your work. One thing (or two) I would add to your list to work on this year would be . . . ." Major on the positive!

Following are some of the kinds of questions you might want to use in a simple evaluation form.
A. Which goals did we reach this year? How?
B. Which goals didn't we reach this year? Why not?
C. Do you understand your job description?
D. Are there any changes needed in the job description?
E. Do you know what is expected of you during the next six months?
F. Describe those aspects of your ministry performance which contribute most to your effectiveness.
G. Describe those aspects of your ministry performance in which improvement would lead to greater effectiveness.
H. What are the most important things for you to be doing in your work? Prioritize from 1-10.
I. What kind of help do you need during the next year?
J. Are there any changes coming in your area you ought to know about? (The leader will need to answer this question.)
K. Are there any changes in your responsibilities? (The leader will need to answer this question.)
L. What are your goals for the next six months (year)?

A second way you can help with reviewing ones work is by being sure each worker fills out the last page of the Ministry/Project Planner (see chapter 7) on anything that person is in charge of. This is a simple evaluation form that can be used as described above. Have the person fill out a copy and share the review with you at the conclusion of the project or program. Any praise or suggestions you have can then be added to what has already been noted. The worker can then observe how to do a better job the next time.

Dealing With Poor Performance

Another area related to this is what do you do when a person is failing in his job, and there are nine months before review time. This person may be doing things in a way destructive to the ministry, or in a way other than agreed upon together with the supervisor. There may be a personality flaw, or the person may simply be a trouble maker. Usually the problem is simply that a good Christian worker is working in an area for which he has no gift or talent. There are a few basics to remember here.
1. You must deal with the situation. It will not go away if you ignore it.
2. You must be honest and yet loving.
3. You may want to consult with the minister or another church leader about the problem for advice and support before speaking with the person.
4. Never correct a person in writing. Always do it face to face. Praise in writing.
5. Don't talk to a bunch of other people about a person behind his back.
6. Don't let a problem go on and on.

Confronting low performance is probably the toughest responsibility to carry out, but the alternative, observed all too frequently, is worse. Unaddressed, chronic, serious difficulty not only demoralizes the organization but undermines an individual's confidence and may make it nearly impossible for the person to bounce back. That's the crime of refusing to act, and act quickly. (Quite simply, nothing reduces the manager's credibility faster than the unwillingness to address an obvious problem. Our people rightly ask, "What . . . is he or she [boss] waiting for?") . . .

Confronting does not mean a tough battle, clash or personal attack, an *unplanned* hostile discussion, browbeating or threatening. It never means treating people badly. Done by the best, it is in no way an opportunity for a frustrated leader to unload on someone else. Confronting is a form of counseling in which the alternatives and consequences are clear and close at hand.[4]

"Low performance" in the church can occur when someone is putting forth no or misdirected effort, has a bad attitude, or is doing more damage than good. Too often in the church, we let situations go on and on where something needs to be done and others are asking, "Why doesn't (the leader of that ministry area) do something about this?"

Mary Kay Ash has written a book on how to deal with people in a business. The basic ideas apply to our work in the church also. She points out the very critical need to deal with negative situations without attacking the worker personally.

I don't think it's ever appropriate for a manager to criticize an individual. Not that criticism should never be given; there are times when a manager must communicate dissatisfaction. But the criticism should be directed at what's wrong—not at who's wrong!

Never giving criticism without praise is a strict rule for me. No matter what you are criticizing, you must find something good to say—both before and after. This is what's known as the "sandwich technique."

Criticize the act, not the person, and try to praise in the beginning and then again after discussing the problem. Also strive to end on a friendly note. By handling the problem this way, you don't subject people to harsh criticism or provoke anger.[5]

Planning Things in Advance

A final suggestion for supporting your partners is to see that each ministry area is planned out well in advance. Most people don't like surprises thrown at them. They like to be able to see where they are going and to know what it will take to get there. That means planning the ministry in advance and showing how each person's role fits into the whole picture.

A car rally is a race in which the drivers do not know in advance what the course will be. There are several checkpoints along the way, and only as the drivers reach these checkpoints do they learn where to go next. It's a lot of fun for a race, but it's no fun at all in ministry.

Uncommon Sightings   PORTLOCK

Big Foot   *Loch Ness Monster*   *Volunteer*

Too many ministries are run like car rallies. The workers perform certain tasks or participate in planned activities with no idea where they will be going next. Only as these tasks or activities are completed do the participants learn what's next. We can support and develop our workers if we help them learn how to picture the whole. To do this, *we* must know where we are going. Then we can share that with the workers and show them how we plan to get there. Then we can tell them how their ministry fits in and help them plan that.

I joined the Arizona Automobile Association this past year. They have a program designed to help members plan trips. I phone them and tell them where I'm going. I tell them whether I want the most direct route, the most scenic route, or the route with the least toll roads—whatever criteria I have for what I want in the trip. In a few days, they provide me with a map showing me exactly where to travel for the trip I described. On the map are noted the locations of restaurants, motels, rest areas, and the like. They even provide a booklet that describes the area around my destination in case I want to do some sightseeing. This is tremendously different from the car-rally approach.

We ought to follow the AAA method of planning our ministries. It builds a person's confidence when he knows exactly where he's going and how to get there. It also makes the ministry more efficient, for the workers can avoid activities that do not help them reach their goal.

Work with your partners in planning a year of ministry in advance. It takes a lot of work, but it is well worth it. Include them in the planning. Avoid doing all the planning yourself and then handing it down to them to carry out for you.

Following is a list of questions you might want to ask your key leaders as they approach a new ministry year:

How do you plan to accomplish the following during this next year in your ministry area?

Communicate your mission to your partners?
Recruit more partners?
Train your partners?
Meet with your partners?
Support and develop your partners?
Honor your partners?
Promote your ministry?
Keep good records?
Gain new prospects for your ministry area?
Follow up on prospects?
Take care of the members of your ministry area?
Follow up on absentees?

Notes

[1]Thomas J. Peters, and Robert H. Waterman, *In Search of Excellence* (New York: Harper and Row, 1984), p. 238.

[2]Callahan, *Twelve Keys*, p. 35.

[3]White, *Excellence in Leadership*, p. 57.

[4]Peters, Austin, *Passion for Excellence*, p. 373.

[5]Mary Kay Ash, *Mary Kay on People Management* (New York: Warner Books, 1984), pp. 37, 38.

Chapter Seven

Planning for Effective Adult Ministry

Students of personality characteristics have always striven to categorize different personality types. Since the days of Hippocrates, one popular system has recognized four types: the melancholy, the sanguine, the choleric, and the phlegmatic. Most psychologists, especially since the time of Freud, reject this system as too simplistic, but it remains popular among many writers. (See, for example, Tim LaHaye, *Transformed Temperaments*, or Florence Littauer, *Personality Plus*.) While granting the simplistic nature of the system, we can still use it to note there are some very real differences among people. These differences are important to note as we consider planning.

Melancholy personality types love to plan. They are detail people; they operate according to a schedule. But not everyone is melancholy; not everyone likes to make plans. Some have the cheerleader enthusiasm of the sanguine personality; others are positive, persuasive, take-charge types who make good leaders—the choleric personality. Finally, there are the laid-back, contented phlegmatics. They make good peacemakers, but they don't care much for extensive planning sessions.

When it comes to planning an activity, a class, or a program for the church, we would be fortunate if we could always have a melancholy personality type in charge. That person will be making his lists and checking them twice. If the event does not come off as a success, it won't be caused by a failure to look ahead. It may fail because there was no cheerleader to promote it, or it might fail because no strong leader emerged to take charge and run with it, but it won't fail from lack of planning.

Often, a program is planned by a person who is more of the sanguine personality type. This person is the rah-rah cheerleader type who can get a lot of people excited about a program and get a big attendance at the first event in the program. But too often, the program turns out to be more hype than substance. The people come the first time because the leader's enthusiasm is contagious, but they will not return to the next event if they do not feel that the first one met any real needs. Behind most successful sanguine types are some melancholy types who take care of the details.

The planning tool in this chapter, the *Ministry/Project Planner*, is designed to help all personality types to be more efficient in considering all the details that must be considered to have an effective event. Sanguines will find it tedious, but they will be more effective if they will use it. The choleric folk will probably have a "better way" and can do it without it, but they, too, will be more efficient if they use it anyway. The melancholy types will be in Hog Heaven. The phlegmatics will say, "Why all the bother?" They'll get tired just looking at it. But it can help them achieve more of their ministry goals. It is designed to help non-detail people think of the details.

As you get familiar with this tool, you will see that many factors go into an event in order to make it a success in terms of reaching its goals. A subtitle for this chapter could be, "Why some good people get good results and others don't." One factor that I believe has caused much unnecessary frustration, discouragement, and disappointment for people working in the church is poor planning. My hope is that this planning tool will help. You still need a lot of enthusiasm, strong leadership, and friendly diplomacy, but without a plan, you more often than not will fail.

Enthusiasm, a lot of prayer, a great idea, or deep commitment do not eliminate the need for good planning. Jesus put it this way.

Suppose one of you wants to build a tower. Will he not first sit down and estimate the cost to see if he has enough money to complete it? For if he lays the foundation and is not able to finish it, everyone who sees it will ridicule him, saying, "This fellow began to build and was not able to finish."

Or suppose a king is about to go to war against another king. Will he not first sit down and consider whether he is able with ten thousand men to oppose the one coming against him with twenty thousand? If he is not able, he will send a delegation while the other is still a long way off and will ask for terms of peace. In the same way, any of you who does not give up everything he has cannot be my disciple (Luke 14:28-33).

In his book on leadership, Fred Smith quotes A. T. Cushman, the CEO of Sears: "The art of administration is constant checking." Smith goes on to elaborate, "He's so right. It's detail work. Managing takes a different set of skills than leading. You lead people, but you manage work."[1] The *Ministry/Project Planner* will give you the means to manage your work and constantly know what to be checking for a given ministry or program.

Some people don't like planning. Some don't think they need to put much into it. I once heard of a person bragging to another that he had the gift of "winging it." Such a gift doesn't exist even though many try and use it. Solid planning is not a luxury for a few; it is a necessity for all. It is not optional.

Captain Russell Grenfell, in *The Bismarck Episode,* wrote: "Every ship's chief officer followed, roughly, this procedure: Analyze the situation as it is and the way in which it developed; visualize all the possibilities; assess them to determine probabilities; estimate the strength of the forces opposed and of our resources; decide upon a general plan; communicate it to those who should know; move to carry out the plan with economy of effort and material; be sure to calculate the chances of prolongation of action; and, most important, shoot at the proper target."[2]

The *Ministry/Project Planner* is designed to help you carry out a similar strategy in your ministries.

Consider a football team again. They start preparing for their next game on Sunday afternoon by watching game films of the game they just played and of the team they will play the next weekend. They have daily classroom sessions to study and lay out their game plan. Dozens of people are involved in the plan. Everyday they have practice on the field to go over the plays for the coming week—trying to correct the errors of the previous week. They lift weights and run and eat and sleep and study all week long. Thousands of hours are put in by the whole team trying to get ready to achieve their goal of a victory. And all of this for just sixty-minutes of football!

If football players put all that into a football game, doesn't our work for the Lord deserve the best game plan we can lay out? The *Ministry/Project Planner* is designed to help you lay out a game plan for a Sunday-school class, a retreat, a special seminar, a conference, or any program. It will help you plan a revival, a volleyball league, or a choir. Try it! You might get to like it!

Right now, take a look at the planning tool (page 65). Note the explanation below. Then look at the completed planning tool beginning on page 51. It shows how the planning tool might be completed to conduct an adult teacher training program using Standard Publishing's *Training Successful Teachers* kit (#18-03204).

Page 1

Write the name of the ministry or project on the blank line.

Page 2

This page begins with identifying who is responsible for the project and attempts to make sure that approval for this project has been given by those who need to authorize it. Once the idea has been approved, it can be planned and implemented. This helps make sure that you have done your homework and have the backing of the church before beginning the ministry or project.

Item 1. The Purpose. Too often we attempt to do things in the church without having a clear understanding as to why we are doing it. This is the starting place. Knowing what your purpose is will affect every other decision you make. You need to know why you are doing the project and for whom. We often fool ourselves in thinking we are doing something for prospects, for example, but then we plan it in light of what we ourselves would like.

Do you need to do some research? Or can this ministry be implemented with what you already know? Over the years, when I have taken on new ministries, I have read everything I could get my hands on about them. I have visited churches who are already doing them well and interview the people responsible. If you are going to do something, find out the best information you can on how to do it.

Item 2. The Picture. The purpose of this section is to get a picture in mind of what the event is to look like. Try to see yourself in the middle of it. What is the atmosphere? What do you see? What do you feel and hear? Now come back to reality: what will it take to make all that happen? What are the measurable results of goals you have in mind? How many do you want there? You need to estimate the attendance because that will effect all other planning.) Who are they? What do you want them to learn, to feel, to experience, or to decide upon? How can you measure whether it happens or not?

Item 3. The Provisions. You are on a retreat, about to show a movie. It's the perfect film to set the retreat off to a good start. You have promoted it. Many people have come, and they are excited. You are pleased with the turnout. You anticipate the effect the movie will have on helping the people grow in the Lord.

You turn the project on, and the movie is underway. And then the bulb burns out! You don't have a spare; the event is over.

That is one common experience that teaches people to think of the things that can mess up a program. Oh, the importance of the details!

The purpose of the Provisions page is to deal with details. It is to help you think of all the little things that need to be anticipated in carrying out a project. You may not need to do everything on this page for every event, but it can jog your memory to be sure and cover all the bases. What resources do you need for your class or event? Try and think of them there. This page will help you anticipate what you need, what it will probably cost, and who will be in charge of taking care of the various tasks. If you find that your name or one other person's name shows up in most all of the "Person in Charge" columns, then it may reveal that you aren't including enough people in the project.

Step 5 is there to help you figure out how much this event is going to cost. Do you have money budgeted for this? Will it cover the anticipated cost of the entire event? If your estimated costs are more than you have budgeted, how will you make up the difference? It is much better to figure this out before an event takes place than to discover at the end that you are hundreds of dollars in the hole.

One lesson I have learned the hard way is to ask people for money in advance. For events that cost, and when you have to make reservations, you'd better get the money up front. What often happens is this: a Sunday-school class wants to go horseback riding. On Sunday, you ask how many want to go. Twenty-five people raise their hands. So on Monday, you call the stables and ask to reserve twenty-five horses at a certain time. But when the anticipated night arrives, only five people show up. You are upset and embarrassed, knowing you have to go to the stables and face the man who just lost money on twenty horses for an hour. You may even have to pay for them. Your fun night just turned sour.

Solve this kind of problem by asking for all money to be paid in advance. Then call the stables. If only five show up, you may still be disappointed, but you don't have to worry about ruining your reputation or the reputation of the church by costing the man a hundred dollars of business. If the people don't show up, they will be out their money, but you aren't out on a limb.

Pages 4 and 5

Pages 4 and 5 are the Provisions Plan Sheets. Here you detail each of the items you checked in the "needed" column on page 3. Steps 1-9 on page four will tell you what to do. See the example.

Page 6: Positions

How many people are you going to need to get the job done? Remember the "baby shower" principle? Don't try and do it all yourself. This page is a worksheet to anticipate the kind of help you need. It also provides a place to figure out how to organize them on a job flow chart. Make a job flow chart to meet your needs. The printed chart may be bigger than you need; if so, leave part of it blank. It may also be too small; add to it or make a separate chart.

A job flow chart can be helpful when recruiting people. It will help them see the big picture.

Page 7: Job Descriptions

Every position on your job flow chart should have a job description made up for it. Every task you need done to carry out your program should show up on someone's job description. Having job descriptions will also help in recruiting. You can show a person what the position is, what the objective is, what specifically that person will be asked to do, whether any experience is needed, what training will be provided, and how you will support the worker while he is performing his job.

Page 8: Proposals

You must plan a recruiting strategy for your event. You may also want to put someone in charge of recruiting for your program other than yourself. Will you want a recruiting tool? How will you approach the people?

There is room on this page to list the positions you need so that you can recruit for them. There is also a place to check to make sure you have a job description before you try and recruit anyone, and a place to list your first choice for the job and then further candidates if that one turns you down.

Page 9: Preparations and Propping

Who will be in charge of training those who've been recruited? Plan your training in advance. This way you can show your recruits exactly how they will be trained.

Your recruited and trained workers need to be backed up. They are your staff. They need to meet together to continue training, for communication, and to be made to feel a part of the team and mission. Determine how you will provide this support. Do you need to send them cards or letters? Do you need to take some of them to lunch? Don't recruit and train them and then abandon them. You may never recruit them for another job.

Page 10: Promotion and Prospects

Who is going to be in charge of selling this project? How will they go about it. Who exactly do you want to participate in the event? How will you get them there? How are you going to beat the drum? You must be creative in the ways you do this. Don't be afraid to use brochures, balloons, bands, and banners. We are often poor promoters in the church. We must do a better job of getting people's attention for our ministries. Nothing works better than personal contact.

Once you get your customers (participants in the event; the ones the ministry is designed to serve) to the event, how will they be treated? How will they be welcomed and involved? What will you be doing to insure that when they leave, they feel that they have been received with genuine care and interest? What can you do to insure they will want to come back again?

Page 11: Picking Up and Plaudits

The section on picking up speaks for itself. There is hardly anything more frustrating than to find yourself all alone after a class, party, or major event, standing in the middle of a major clean up job. One way to avoid that is to plan in advance to take care of it.

As for plaudits, we are too negligent in thanking people for a job well done. Jesus wasn't hesitant about praising people. You must thank, honor, and recognize those who work with you on your project. Yes, some people would rather be left in the dark recesses, faithfully doing their tasks out of love. You honor and recognize them anyway. Use notes, verbal praise, plaques, certificates, and/or gifts as tokens of appreciation. These small investments will make a difference in peoples' attitudes and ministries.

Page 12: Postlude

We are often afraid to evaluate, but we must. We all want to improve and do a better job at most everything in life. That isn't possible without evaluation. This page asks who is going to fill out the form and who will review it with that person. It is good to make sure at the beginning of a project that the leader knows this will be done at the end. You might want all those helping with the project to fill one of these out and have a group evaluation. Evaluations are not intended to tear people down, but to build them up. This gives you the opportunity to praise people for a job well done and to share suggestions as to how they can improve their work or project the next time.

Additional Pointers in Using the *Ministry/Project Planner*

When you are the person in charge of a project, you need to fill out a *Ministry/Project Planner* on the overall project. As you recruit leaders for various tasks within the overall project, fill out planners on the tasks they are doing. You need to start this process far enough in advance of your project so you can meet with your leaders, show them what they need to do, brainstorm with them, and then ask them to complete their forms and report back. If a person isn't able or interested in doing his part of the project in advance, then you will have time to discover that.

You may say, "This has to be done by next Tuesday." If someone does not have it done and will not cooperate, then you may simply have to give the job to another person. You could say, "I have to have this done, and apparently this is a bad time for you to be able to do it. I'll find someone else who can do it now. If you later see you'll be able to help, let me know and we'll find another job for you." The tool gives you a way to find out who the reliable workers are, and to move the ones who just won't do what is needed to see the ministry achieve its goals.

Notes

[1]Fred Smith, *Learning to Lead* (Waco: Word, 1986), p. 31.

[2]Callahan, *Twelve Keys*, p. 62.

MINISTRY / PROJECT
PLANNER
BY JOHN HENDEE

For **Adult Teacher Training Program**
Ministry/Project

MINISTRY / PROJECT PLANNER

FOR _Adult Teacher Training Program_
Ministry / Project

Person responsible for this project _Steve Johnson, Adult S.S. Superintendent_
Name

This has been approved to implement and carry out by
Mark Johnson, C.E. Director   _6/5/89_
Name   Date

1. The PURPOSE of this ministry is: _To train ten (10) new adult S.S. Teachers by January 1, 1990_

Does this support your group's mission? _Yes_

Who are you doing this for? (Target group) _Adults willing to teach an adult S.S. Class_

Desired Benefits	Possible Problems	Suggested Solutions
To have 10 new teachers to help in 6 classes by 1/1/90 and have 4 backups	_Not recruiting enough, and their being ready by 1/1/90_	_We've started early_

Research to be done? (reading, interviews, visits, etc.)

What?	By Whom?	When?
A. _Read Hendee's book on recruiting & training adult workers_	_Mark / Steve_	_Finish by 6/10/89_
B. _Interview 2 other C.E. Dir._	_Mark/Steve & Trainers_	_Finish by 6/10/89_
C. _Examine Standard Publishing materials - TRAINING SUCCESSFUL TEACHERS_	_Mark/Steve & Trainers_	_Finish by 6/10/89_

2. The PICTURE of this ministry. What are the expected, measurable results and goals?

Have 6 more teachers ready to teach 6 new classes by December 1

Have 4 other teachers ready to replace the current ones needing to stop. We'll use them as back-ups and subs. until needed in regular class.

ESTIMATED ATTENDANCE? _Goal — 12_

3. The PROVISIONS for this Ministry.

    Step 1. Look at the items in the "needed" column and check off those you need to carry out this ministry.

    Step 2. Write down who will be responsible for each area.

    Step 3. Complete pages 4-12.

    Step 4. Fill in the cost column for each area as it is determined.

Check if needed			Person Responsible	Estimated Cost
	1. PROVISIONS			
X	a.	Master calendar checked	Jane	⎯
X	b.	Location, rooms reserved	Jane	⎯
X	c.	Equipment reserved	Jane	⎯
	d.	Deposits made		
X	e.	Food preparation	Susan	$20.00
	f.	Transportation needs		
X	g.	Program planned	Joe	⎯
X	h.	Program schedule printed	Jane	10.00
X	i.	Curriculum needs	Joe	see #4 below
X	j.	Speakers, teachers	Joe	see #4 below
X	k.	Printing needs	Jane	see #4 below
X	l.	Directions, maps, signs	Jane	5.00
	m.	Permission slips		
X	n.	Greeters	David	⎯
	o.	Music needs		
X	p.	Registrations	David	5.00
	q.	Supplies		
X	r.	Babysitting arranged	Jane	50.00
	s.	Insurance		
	t.	Parking needs		
	u.	Set-up		
	v.	Other		
X	2. POSITIONS Plan Sheet (pages 6 & 7)		Steve	
X	3. PROPOSALS -- Recruiting (page 8)		Karen	20.00
X	4. PREPARATIONS -- Training (page 9)		Joe	170.95
X	5. PROPPING -- Supporting Partners (page 9)		Steve	0.00
X	6. PROMOTION -- Selling it (page 10)		Karen	5.00
X	7. PROSPECTS for this Ministry (page 10)		Karen/David	10.00
X	8. PICKING UP -- (page 11)		Joe	⎯
X	9. PLAUDITS & Recognition (page 11)		Steve	32.00
X	10. POSTLUDE -- Evaluation (page 12)		Steve/Mark	⎯
			TOTAL Estimated Cost	337.95

Step 5. a. Amount budgeted for this: ___$400.00___

       b. Total estimated cost for this: ___375.95___

       c. If "b" is larger than "a", how will you fund the difference?_____

PROVISIONS Plan Sheet

Step 1. Place the letter (a, b, etc.) of the first item checked "needed" (on page 3) in column 1.
Step 2. List anything that needs to be done to carry out that item in column 2.
Step 3. Prioritize with numbers (1, 2, etc.) all the steps of this item in column 3.
Step 4. Put in the estimated cost of each item in column 4.
Step 5. Write in the start date for each step in column 5.
Step 6. Write in the finish date for each step in column 6.
Step 7. Write in the name of the person in charge of each step in column 7.
Step 8. Check off each step in column 8 when it has been completed.
Step 9. Copy each amount in the "estimated cost" column on page 3.

1 INSERT LETTER OF ITEM	2 STEPS TO BE TAKEN	3 PRIORITIZE	4 EST. COST	5 START DATE	6 FINISH DATE	7 PERSON IN CHARGE	8 CHECK WHEN FINISHED
a	Ck./w/Kim to make sure there are no conflicts with date. Get on calendar for November 12	1 / 2			4-8-89 / 4-8-89	Steve / "	
b	Reserve room & kitchen	1			4-8-89	Steve	
c	Reserve overhead, record player & filmstrip projector				4-8-89	Steve	
e	Plan snacks / Pick up food / Get supplies to serve / Get helper		$20.		9-1-89 / " / " / "	Susan / " / " / "	
g	Plan topic to cover / Materials to use / Order materials / Set time agenda	1 / 3 / 4 / 2			5-1-89 / / 7-1-89 / "	Joe / " / " / "	
h	Get program from Joe / Type and print	1 / 2	$10.		8-1-89	Jane / "	
i	Order 12 copies of text & kit book from Standard				5-1-89	Joe	

PROVISIONS Plan Sheet # 2

1 INSERT LETTER OF ITEM	2 STEPS TO BE TAKEN	3 PRIOR-ITIZE	4 EST. COST	5 START DATE transfer dates to permanent calendar	6 FINISH DATE	7 PERSON IN CHARGE	8 CHECK WHEN FINISHED
j	Line up guest teacher/trainer				5-1-89	Joe	
k	See what Joe & guest trainer need printed				9-1-89	Jane	
l	Make posters for campus showing location		$5.		10-1-89	Jane	
n	Have name tags made up — arrive early to greet & introduce people (use tags that we now have				11-15-89	David	
p	Have registration cards ready	1	$5.		9-1-89	Steve	
	Registration table set up for three weeks prior	2			11-1-89	"	
r	Line up two babysitters				9-1-89	Jane	
	Contact sitters				10-1-89	"	
	Make up P.O. to pay sitters		$50.		10-1-89	"	
u	Set up room & materials & equipment				12-3-89	Joe	

POSITIONS Plan Sheet

Step 1. List all the possible working positions you will need to carry out this ministry/project. Look at the "Person Responsible" column on page 3 for possible positions needed.

Step 2. Design a job flow chart organizing all of your needed positions.

LIST ALL THE POSITIONS NEEDED FOR THIS MINISTRY:
(See "Person Responsible" column on page 3)

Refreshments/food   Trainer

Registration

Recruitment

Training format

Secretarial duties

Greeting

DESIGN A JOB FLOW CHART

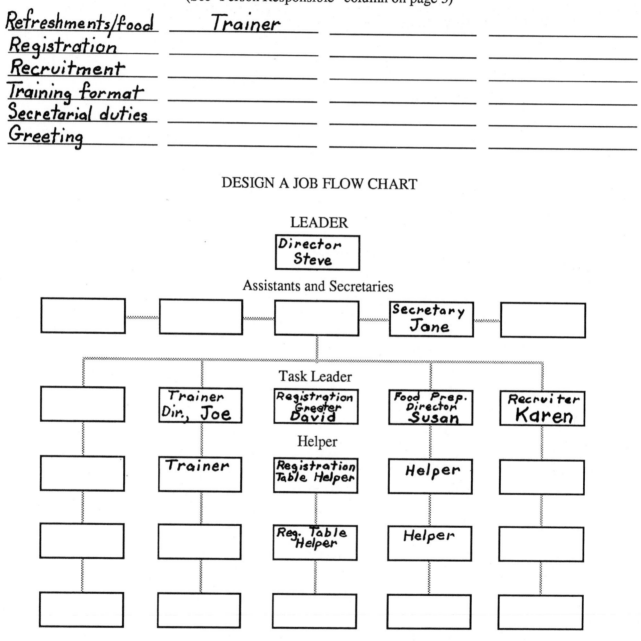

JOB DESCRIPTIONS

Step 1. Fill out a job analysis section for each job position on your job flow chart. Every task or assignment on pages 3-5 should show up on someone's job description.

POSITION: Director - Steve	**POSITION:** Secretary - Jane	**POSITION:** Training Dir. - Joe
OBJECTIVE:	**OBJECTIVE:**	**OBJECTIVE:**
SPECIFIC RESPONSIBILITIES: Call & lead meetings Recruit Staff Plan master Calendar for event Organize staff for training	**SPECIFIC RESPONSIBILITIES:** Babysitters Ck. Calendar Reserve rooms/nursery/kitchen/overhead/movie Print program Order texts. Draw maps	**SPECIFIC RESPONSIBILITIES:** Outline training Agenda Line up teachers/trainers Order materials Set up the rooms Chalkboards/Overhead/Proj.
EXPERIENCE NEEDED:	**EXPERIENCE NEEDED:**	**EXPERIENCE NEEDED:** Meet Director
TRAINING PROVIDED:	**TRAINING PROVIDED:**	**TRAINING PROVIDED:**
SUPPORT TO BE GIVEN:	**SUPPORT TO BE GIVEN:** Weekly meeting/use of equip. & supplies	**SUPPORT TO BE GIVEN:**
POSITION: Registrar/Greeter David	**POSITION:** Food Prep. Dir. Susan	**POSITION:** Recruiter - Karen
OBJECTIVE:	**OBJECTIVE:**	**OBJECTIVE:**
SPECIFIC RESPONSIBILITIES: Oversee registration table for 3 weeks Name tags Get greeters to session early	**SPECIFIC RESPONSIBILITIES:** Plan snack food Supplies Helpers	**SPECIFIC RESPONSIBILITIES:** Make up flyer Poster Letters Phone calls/visits Information booth
EXPERIENCE NEEDED:	**EXPERIENCE NEEDED:**	**EXPERIENCE NEEDED:**
TRAINING PROVIDED:	**TRAINING PROVIDED:**	**TRAINING PROVIDED:**
SUPPORT TO BE GIVEN:	**SUPPORT TO BE GIVEN:** $_____ use of kitchen	**SUPPORT TO BE GIVEN:** Weekly meetings / Supplies
POSITION:	**POSITION:**	**POSITION:**
OBJECTIVE:	**OBJECTIVE:**	**OBJECTIVE:**
SPECIFIC RESPONSIBILITIES:	**SPECIFIC RESPONSIBILITIES:**	**SPECIFIC RESPONSIBILITIES:**
EXPERIENCE NEEDED:	**EXPERIENCE NEEDED:**	**EXPERIENCE NEEDED:**
TRAINING PROVIDED:	**TRAINING PROVIDED:**	**TRAINING PROVIDED:**
SUPPORT TO BE GIVEN:	**SUPPORT TO BE GIVEN:**	**SUPPORT TO BE GIVEN:**

PROPOSALS - Recruiting Your Partners

Step 1. Who is in charge? __Steve__

Step 2. What tool will be used to recruit? __Brochure made by Jane__

Step 3. What is your recruiting strategy or plan? __Select names; prayer week; letter sent out; home visits to candidates__

Step 4. When will this be done? __September '89__

Step 5. What will this cost? __$20.00 for Brochure__ (Record also on page 3.)

Step 6. List the positions and people you will be seeking to recruit.

Check when Recruited	Positions	Have Job Description?	Prospect #1	Prospect #2	Prospect #3	Prospect #4
X	Recruiter	yes	Karen			
X	Secretary	yes	Jane			
X	Trainer	yes	Joe			
X	Registrar	yes	David			
	Food Prep.	yes	Susan			
	Teacher	yes	Michael			
	Teacher	yes	Cecil			
	Teacher	yes	Marion			
	Teacher	yes	Tom H.			
	Teacher	yes	Roy			
	Teacher	yes	Tom L.			
	Teacher	yes	Doug			
	Teacher	yes	Don A.			
	Teacher	yes	Don T.			
	Teacher	yes	Karen			
	Teacher	yes	Bill			
	Teacher	yes	Judy			

PREPARATIONS - Training your partners

Step 1. Who is in charge? _Joe_

Step 2. Who needs to be trained? _12 candidates to be recruited_

Step 3. What are the goals of the training? _To have ten teachers ready to teach January 1, 1990 by taking them through Standard's TRAINING SUCCESSFUL TEACHERS_

Step 4. When will it take place? _December 4-5, 1989 - Friday P.M. & Saturday A.M._

Step 5. Where? _Church - Room 14A & Kitchen & Nursery_

Step 6. Outline the training.

	What will you need to do this?	Cost?
1. _Jesus The Master Teacher_	_1 TRAINING SUCCESSFUL TEACHERS Kit_	$49.95
2. _Teach the Bible for Results_		
3. _A Christian Basis for Devel._	_2 Instructor Books_	_10.00_
4. _Looking for a Map to Success_	_12 Student Books_	_36.00_
5. _Maintain Classroom Control_	_Honorarium for Trainer_	_75.00_
6. _A Question of Method_		

Total $170.95

Record TOTAL cost on page 3

PROPPING - Supporting Your Partners

Step 1. Who is in charge? _Steve_

Step 2. Whom do you need to support?
Current Existing Teachers
New Teachers
Training Committee

Step 3. How do you plan to support them? (mailings, meetings, personal contact, etc.)

	What will you need to do this?	Cost?
Monthly letter		_$10. ($120. per. yr.)_
Quarterly meal-Guest speaker		_Dutch meals_
Monthly teacher meeting		—
Ck. w/new teachers by phone wkly.		—
Visit their class		—

Total $10.00

Record TOTAL cost on page 3

PROMOTION - How Will You Sell This Ministry?

Step 1. Who is in charge? _Karen_

Step 2. Who is the "target group"? Whom do you want to "sell" on this project? _12 names we want to recruit_

Step 3. What is your "selling" strategy or plan?

What is your "selling" strategy or plan?	What do you need to do this?	Cost?
Send intro. letter to 12	Postage, letters, envelopes	$5.00
Phone to set up home visit		
Show them our brochure/		
ask to attend training		
prayer week of prayer		
	TOTAL	$5.00

Record TOTAL cost on page 3

PROSPECTS For This Ministry

Step 1. Who is in charge of this? _Karen / David_

Step 2. Who are your "customers"? Whom do you want to serve with this ministry?
The "customers" will be the 12 recruits who attend the training

What is your step by step plan for insuring that your customers are taken care of?	What will you need to do this?	Cost?
Greeter/Name tags		$5.00
Name on their notebooks		4.00
Name place cards		1.00
Intro. all to the other -		
Share backgrounds		
Assign long time		
members to host		
newer teacher		
candidates		
	TOTAL	$10.00

Record TOTAL cost on page 3

PICKING UP - How Will You Clean Up Afterward?

Step 1. Who is in charge of clean up procedure? __Joe__

Step 2. When will it be done? __Immediately after last session__

Step 3.

What will need to be done?	What will you need to do this?	Cost?
Re-arrange room	David	
Return equipment	Joe	
Check that nursery is neat & clean	Jane	
Check that kitchen is neat & clean	Susan	
Return all training materials to office	Steve	
	TOTAL	−0−

Record TOTAL cost on page 3

PLAUDITS - How Will You Recognize and Honor Your Partners?

Step 1. Who is in charge? __Steve__

Step 2.

How will you recognize or honor your partners?	What will you need to do this?	Cost?
Send thank you cards	Cards & Pen	$2.00
Recognize them at training	Plan a time to do this/lunch	
Put things in newsletters	Write short article	
Invite staff to appreciation banquet		
Have wrap-up dinner at a home to do evaluation		30.00
	TOTAL	32.00

Record TOTAL cost on page 3

Step 3. When will this be done?

__December 10 Friday night /Steve   6:30 P.M.__

Step 4. Where will this be done?

__At Steve's house__

POSTLUDE
Evaluating This Ministry

Evaluation will be reviewed with whom? _Mark_

When? _December 15, 1989_

Step 1. Completed by _Steve_

Step 2. Did this Ministry/Project achieve its goals? If yes, how? _____

Step 3. What went right? _____

Step 4. What would you do differently next time? _____

Step 5. Evaluate on the scale below how the various stages of the ministry went.

Weak . . . . Strong

PROVISIONS	1	2	3	4	5	6	7	8	9	10
POSITIONS	1	2	3	4	5	6	7	8	9	10
PROPOSALS	1	2	3	4	5	6	7	8	9	10
PREPARATIONS	1	2	3	4	5	6	7	8	9	10
PROPPING	1	2	3	4	5	6	7	8	9	10
PROMOTION	1	2	3	4	5	6	7	8	9	10
PROSPECTS	1	2	3	4	5	6	7	8	9	10
PICKING UP	1	2	3	4	5	6	7	8	9	10
PLAUDITS	1	2	3	4	5	6	7	8	9	10

Any other comments _____

The *Ministry/Project Planner* on the following pages (65-76) is provided for your convenience. It is perforated for easy removal from the book, and you, as a purchaser of this book, may make as many copies of it as you need for noncommercial use in your own church or church program. However, according to U.S. Copyright Law, no other portion of this book may be copied in any way without written permission from the publisher.

MINISTRY / PROJECT
PLANNER
BY JOHN HENDEE

For_____
Ministry/Project

MINISTRY / PROJECT PLANNER

FOR _____
Ministry / Project

Person responsible for this project _____
Name

This has been approved to implement and carry out by

_____
Name   Date

1. The PURPOSE of this ministry is:_____
_____

Does this support your group's mission?_____

Who are you doing this for? (Target group)_____

Desired Benefits	Possible Problems	Suggested Solutions
_____	_____	_____
_____	_____	_____
_____	_____	_____
_____	_____	_____

Research to be done? (reading, interviews, visits, etc.)

What?	By Whom?	When?
_____	_____	_____
_____	_____	_____
_____	_____	_____
_____	_____	_____
_____	_____	_____
_____	_____	_____

2. The PICTURE of this ministry. What are the expected, measurable results and goals?

_____	_____
_____	_____
_____	_____
_____	_____
_____	_____
_____	_____

ESTIMATED ATTENDANCE? _____

3. The PROVISIONS for this Ministry.
   Step 1. Look at the items in the "needed" column and check off those you need to carry out this ministry.
   Step 2. Write down who will be responsible for each area.
   Step 3. Complete pages 4-12.
   Step 4. Fill in the cost column for each area as it is determined.

Check if needed		Person Responsible	Estimated Cost
	1. PROVISIONS		
	a. Master calendar checked		
	b. Location, rooms reserved		
	c. Equipment reserved		
	d. Deposits made		
	e. Food preparation		
	f. Transportation needs		
	g. Program planned		
	h. Program schedule printed		
	i. Curriculum needs		
	j. Speakers, teachers		
	k. Printing needs		
	l. Directions, maps, signs		
	m. Permission slips		
	n. Greeters		
	o. Music needs		
	p. Registrations		
	q. Supplies		
	r. Babysitting arranged		
	s. Insurance		
	t. Parking needs		
	u. Set-up		
	v. Other		
	2. POSITIONS Plan Sheet (pages 6 & 7)		
	3. PROPOSALS -- Recruiting (page 8)		
	4. PREPARATIONS -- Training (page 9)		
	5. PROPPING -- Supporting Partners (page 9)		
	6. PROMOTION -- Selling it (page 10)		
	7. PROSPECTS for this Ministry (page 10)		
	8. PICKING UP -- (page 11)		
	9. PLAUDITS & Recognition (page 11)		
	10. POSTLUDE -- Evaluation (page 12)		
	TOTAL Estimated Cost		

Step 5. a. Amount budgeted for this: _____

   b. Total estimated cost for this: _____

   c. If "b" is larger than "a", how will you fund the difference?_____

_____

PROVISIONS Plan Sheet

Step 1. Place the letter (a, b, etc.) of the first item checked "needed" (on page 3) in column 1.
Step 2. List anything that needs to be done to carry out that item in column 2.
Step 3. Prioritize with numbers (1, 2, etc.) all the steps of this item in column 3.
Step 4. Put in the estimated cost of each item in column 4.
Step 5. Write in the start date for each step in column 5.
Step 6. Write in the finish date for each step in column 6.
Step 7. Write in the name of the person in charge of each step in column 7.
Step 8. Check off each step in column 8 when it has been completed.
Step 9. Copy each amount in the "estimated cost" column on page 3.

1	2	3	4	5	6	7	8
INSERT LETTER OF ITEM	STEPS TO BE TAKEN	PRIOR-ITIZE	EST. COST	START DATE transfer dates to permanent calendar	FINISH DATE	PERSON IN CHARGE	CHECK WHEN FINISHED

PROVISIONS Plan Sheet # 2

1	2	3	4	5	6	7	8
INSERT LETTER OF ITEM	STEPS TO BE TAKEN	PRIOR-ITIZE	EST. COST	START DATE	FINISH DATE	PERSON IN CHARGE	CHECK WHEN FINISHED
				transfer dates to permanent calendar			

POSITIONS Plan Sheet

Step 1. List all the possible working positions you will need to carry out this ministry/project. Look at the "Person Responsible" column on page 3 for possible positions needed.

Step 2. Design a job flow chart organizing all of your needed positions.

LIST ALL THE POSITIONS NEEDED FOR THIS MINISTRY:
(See "Person Responsible" column on page 3)

DESIGN A JOB FLOW CHART

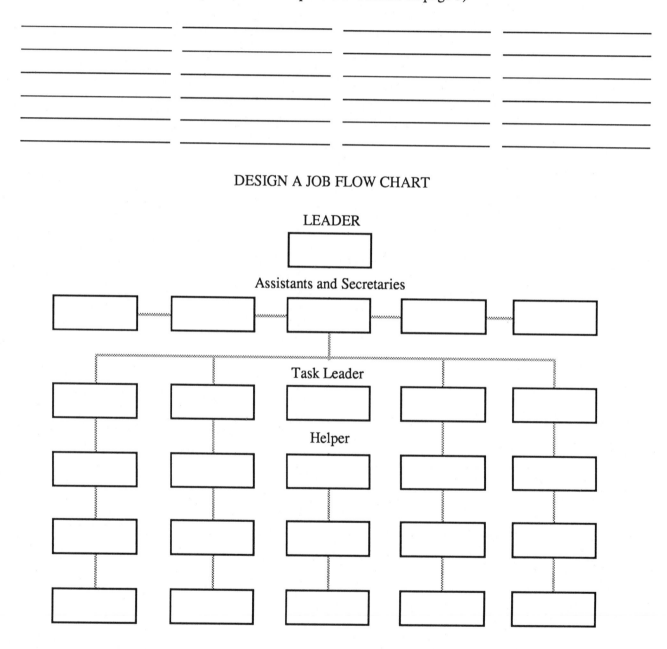

JOB DESCRIPTIONS

Step 1. Fill out a job analysis section for each job position on your job flow chart. Every task or assignment on pages 3-5 should show up on someone's job description.

POSITION: **OBJECTIVE:** **SPECIFIC RESPONSIBILITIES:** **EXPERIENCE NEEDED:** **TRAINING PROVIDED:** **SUPPORT TO BE GIVEN:**	**POSITION:** **OBJECTIVE:** **SPECIFIC RESPONSIBILITIES:** **EXPERIENCE NEEDED:** **TRAINING PROVIDED:** **SUPPORT TO BE GIVEN:**	**POSITION:** **OBJECTIVE:** **SPECIFIC RESPONSIBILITIES:** **EXPERIENCE NEEDED:** **TRAINING PROVIDED:** **SUPPORT TO BE GIVEN:**
POSITION: **OBJECTIVE:** **SPECIFIC RESPONSIBILITIES:** **EXPERIENCE NEEDED:** **TRAINING PROVIDED:** **SUPPORT TO BE GIVEN:**	**POSITION:** **OBJECTIVE:** **SPECIFIC RESPONSIBILITIES:** **EXPERIENCE NEEDED:** **TRAINING PROVIDED:** **SUPPORT TO BE GIVEN:**	**POSITION:** **OBJECTIVE:** **SPECIFIC RESPONSIBILITIES:** **EXPERIENCE NEEDED:** **TRAINING PROVIDED:** **SUPPORT TO BE GIVEN:**
POSITION: **OBJECTIVE:** **SPECIFIC RESPONSIBILITIES:** **EXPERIENCE NEEDED:** **TRAINING PROVIDED:** **SUPPORT TO BE GIVEN:**	**POSITION:** **OBJECTIVE:** **SPECIFIC RESPONSIBILITIES:** **EXPERIENCE NEEDED:** **TRAINING PROVIDED:** **SUPPORT TO BE GIVEN:**	**POSITION:** **OBJECTIVE:** **SPECIFIC RESPONSIBILITIES:** **EXPERIENCE NEEDED:** **TRAINING PROVIDED:** **SUPPORT TO BE GIVEN:**

PROPOSALS - Recruiting Your Partners

Step 1. Who is in charge? _____

Step 2. What tool will be used to recruit? _____

Step 3. What is your recruiting strategy or plan? _____

_____

_____

Step 4. When will this be done? _____

Step 5. What will this cost? _____ (Record also on page 3.)

Step 6. List the positions and people you will be seeking to recruit. _____

_____

Check when Recruited	Positions	Have Job Description?	Prospect #1	Prospect #2	Prospect #3	Prospect #4

PREPARATIONS - Training your partners

Step 1. Who is in charge? _____

Step 2. Who needs to be trained? _____

_____

Step 3. What are the goals of the training? _____

_____

_____

Step 4. When will it take place? _____

Step 5. Where? _____

Step 6. Outline the training.   What will you need to do this?   Cost?

_____	_____	_____
_____	_____	_____
_____	_____	_____
_____	_____	_____
_____	_____	_____
_____	_____	_____

Total _____

Record TOTAL cost on page 3

PROPPING - Supporting Your Partners

Step 1. Who is in charge? _____

Step 2. Whom do you need to support?

_____	_____	_____
_____	_____	_____
_____	_____	_____
_____	_____	_____

Step 3.   How do you plan to support them?   What will you need to do this?   Cost?
(mailings, meetings, personal contact, etc.)

_____	_____	_____
_____	_____	_____
_____	_____	_____
_____	_____	_____
_____	_____	_____
_____	_____	_____
_____	_____	_____

Total _____

Record TOTAL cost on page 3

PROMOTION - How Will You Sell This Ministry?

Step 1. Who is in charge? _____

Step 2. Who is the "target group"? Whom do you want to "sell" on this project? _____
_____

Step 3. What is your "selling" strategy or plan?	What do you need to do this?	Cost?
_____	_____	_____
_____	_____	_____
_____	_____	_____
_____	_____	_____
_____	_____	_____
_____	_____	_____
	TOTAL	_____

Record TOTAL cost on page 3

PROSPECTS For This Ministry

Step 1. Who is in charge of this? _____

Step 2. Who are your "customers"? Whom do you want to serve with this ministry?

_____

What is your step by step plan for insuring that your customers are taken care of?	What will you need to do this?	Cost?
_____	_____	_____
_____	_____	_____
_____	_____	_____
_____	_____	_____
_____	_____	_____
_____	_____	_____
_____	_____	_____
_____	_____	_____
_____	_____	_____
_____	_____	_____
	TOTAL	_____

Record TOTAL cost on page 3

PICKING UP - How Will You Clean Up Afterward?

Step 1. Who is in charge of clean up procedure?_____
_____

Step 2. When will it be done?_____

Step 3.

What will need to be done?	What will you need to do this?	Cost?
_____	_____	_____
_____	_____	_____
_____	_____	_____
_____	_____	_____
_____	_____	_____
_____	_____	_____
	TOTAL	_____

Record TOTAL cost on page 3

PLAUDITS - How Will You Recognize and Honor Your Partners?

Step 1. Who is in charge? _____

Step 2.

How will you recognize or honor your partners?	What will you need to do this?	Cost?
_____	_____	_____
_____	_____	_____
_____	_____	_____
_____	_____	_____
_____	_____	_____
	TOTAL	_____

Record TOTAL cost on page 3

Step 3. When will this be done?
_____
_____
_____
_____
_____

Step 4. Where will this be done?
_____
_____
_____

POSTLUDE
Evaluating This Ministry

Evaluation will be reviewed with whom?_____
_____

When? _____
_____

Step 1. Completed by _____
_____

Step 2. Did this Ministry/Project achieve its goals? If yes, how? _____
_____
_____
_____

Step 3. What went right?_____
_____
_____
_____

Step 4. What would you do differently next time?_____
_____
_____
_____
_____

Step 5. Evaluate on the scale below how the various stages of the ministry went.

Weak . . . . Strong

PROVISIONS.	1	2	3	4	5	6	7	8	9	10
POSITIONS	1	2	3	4	5	6	7	8	9	10
PROPOSALS.	1	2	3	4	5	6	7	8	9	10
PREPARATIONS.	1	2	3	4	5	6	7	8	9	10
PROPPING.	1	2	3	4	5	6	7	8	9	10
PROMOTION.	1	2	3	4	5	6	7	8	9	10
PROSPECTS.	1	2	3	4	5	6	7	8	9	10
PICKING UP.	1	2	3	4	5	6	7	8	9	10
PLAUDITS.	1	2	3	4	5	6	7	8	9	10

Any other comments _____
_____
_____
_____
_____
_____
_____
_____
_____